THE SANE GAME

Sarah L. Drury

For

My beloved husband John, my soulmate in heaven;
My earth-angel mother, Jennifer Cranidge;
My two sisters, Sinead and Corrina, who have showed me
unconditional love;
My grandparents, who I hope are looking down from their heavenly
sofas and smiling;
Carol Crawley, my heaven-sent and dearest friend;
Sara Long, my long suffering CPN, always there with a smile and a
comforting word;
My darling niece, Esmai, who shines like the sun,

And finally,

My beautiful son Milo, the brightest star in the universe,
Who lights up every moment of my life
And always will.

'This Morn'

This morn, the sun forgot to rise,
A velvet, grey, nightmare moment,
Web of 'no I cannot do this day' once more,
Beneath plump duvets of obscurity.

This morn, the clock just laughed,
A hollow, crazy cackle,
Random, scattered moments painted on
A timeless life-machine.

This morn, her mind just broke,
Innumerable insane fragments,
Shattered, broken remnants, looking,
Grasping at insanity.

© *Sarah Drury*

ONE

I remember when it all began. The madness. I was a happily single girl with a successful career. A primary school teacher, passionately shaping young minds, in a well-respected school in a desirable and terribly chic suburb of Manchester. I was a quirky young thing, independent and feisty. Creativity possessed me day in, day out, and my life was a whirl of music and art and passion. I juggled my day job with nights and weekends performing with the Halle Choir, my voice resplendent with joy as the music rang through the ethers. Oh, those were indeed happy times, heady heights to fall from. Life was so good.

Then Bang! I woke up one morning and I knew not what had hit me. My happy had vanished. My world as I had known it had been torn apart. I had every intention of getting up, going to teach the kids, the normal routine, but for some reason I could do nothing. Except cry. I could cry well, in fact. And cry I did. And didn't stop. I lay there on the bare wooden floorboards, between beautiful sea green walls, clutching the phone and pleading for help of any sort. I was lucky that day. I had an angel for a friend, who reached out to me in my darkest hour. And so began my descent into the world of the mentally ill.

It was the GP who referred me to the local psychiatric hospital. Withington Hospital was a forbidding place. A huge, Victorian style building, the godforsaken sort of nightmare you would see in a horror film. A sobbing wreck, I took my first steps into my new-found world of psychiatry. I was absolutely terrified. Mental institutions were things I had only read about in books or seen in films. Surreal and archaic full of sadistic doctors. There was no privacy, no dignity in this place. I had my own bed, sure, though the hospital issue curtain, whilst providing a modicum of privacy, never really promised to protect me from the sick people. But I would learn, boy would I learn, that I was at one with them in this sea of insanity.

I never had a diagnosis back then, I don't think the doctors knew how to label me. I was certainly very depressed, but also deeply disturbed. My own mind was tormenting me, punishing me, torturing me. I had been plunged into the darkest depths of depression, but my mind just would not be still. I was being harassed every waking second by my own psyche! These were the darkest of days and the most confused.

I was very scared, surrounded by madness. I had always heard the tales of my great grandmother, who had suffered psychosis and depression and endured the hell that was the asylum, back in the days of unmodified Electro Convulsive Therapy and hydro treatments. Barbaric! She lived to tell the tale. But this was my first forage into the world of psychiatry. I hid away at first, in psychological torment and not wanting to be a part of it. I sought sanctuary behind the curtains of my bed space and tried to block out reality, although the boundaries of the real and unreal have no clarity in the world of the mentally ill. I lived for the fleeting visits from friends and family, for the moments when I ventured out of the ward and into the therapy rooms. I just wanted escape. Not just from the institution but from existing in this torturous mind and body.

I spent an awful lot of time lying on the floor in a mental stupor being ignored by the nurses. I must've looked an arresting sight with my hospital gown and unwashed hair, sprawling across the corridor. I was so desperate, so tortured. My mind was broken and screaming for sanctity. It was hell. And their diagnosis? They didn't know how to help me. I had psychological issues. I was an attention seeker. For God's sake, I had been a teacher, a singer, a musician, in the public eye. Why the hell would I want more attention, and why on earth would I really wish to be on a floor, crying and screaming, in mental agony, when I could be living a normal existence?

Days were spent in the dayroom and the art therapy rooms. Then one day I met Josie. Josie was manic depressive (so it was called back then) and fluctuated between being perfectly lucid to being wildly psychotic and paranoid. She was a slight, frail woman with dirty-blonde, unkempt hair who would frequent the dayroom, her nicotine-stained fingers clutching at the remains of a cigarette. She was nervous and unpredictable. Vulnerable, even. I tried so hard to be friends. We used to laugh and joke in her milder moments and talk about her hopes and plans for the future. We shared smokes and dreams. She had been having an illicit affair with a younger guy who had a family and she desperately wanted him to leave his wife. She confided in me and I listened and didn't judge, for I wasn't a judgmental sort of person back then (I think that comes later!). We shared our sorrows and secrets, and all was good. For a while.

Then one afternoon I went into the dayroom to greet my new friend and all hell broke loose. She launched herself into a fiery, furious tirade of abuse, screaming and shouting, swearing and cursing. I was not to be trusted, I was evil and twisted. I had been turning her boyfriend against her, apparently and spreading nasty rumours. My new friend had turned against me, through no fault of her own. Her paranoia and psychosis had taken a firm hold, and she was convinced I was evil incarnate. She was furious with me and I didn't understand. I had not thought of her as a woman with a mental illness, I had not judged her at all. And I was naive in this world of madness, I had very little knowledge of mental illness and absolutely no experience. I had never encountered people in a psychosis or a bout of paranoia or mania before. It was a shock to my system and it was very hard to be objective. I took the situation and turned it in on myself. I was mortified and the seeming rejection by a fellow patient added to my frail psychological state. I simply could not deal with what had happened and again my world fell apart. I wanted to rip out my hair and pull out my teeth, I wanted to be a vehicle for pain and stop hurting all at the same time. I threw myself into a tangled, wailing heap on the floor, huge sobs and cries flooding the ward. I must have been a spectacle, lying on the floor in the day room, sobbing and screaming. Baring my woes to those who had woes of their own. Another crazy lady adding to the mixture of psychological liquorice allsorts.

It was in this state that I finally cracked and made a bid for freedom. My very good friend had come to visit and she was an experienced psychiatric nurse. I trusted her with my life. She happened to walk through the door as all hell broke loose and I was causing pandemonium. Of course, none of the nurses knew what had happened with Josie's psychosis and how much it had distressed me so they treated me with disdain, as they had done all along. They just saw this out of control, crazily distressed 'drama queen' and paid little attention. They had no way of knowing just how much psychological agony I was in and how fractured my mind was. I had been treated very badly the whole time. Left lying distressed on the floor in the corridors, treated as though I was an inconvenience. I got to the point where I just exploded and decided I had to get out of that place and fast. I ran to the doors just as my good friend walked in and she was utterly shocked at the dramatic scene that greeted her. I knew I had to leave and the nurses didn't really try to stop me. I walked away from that hospital in a worse state than when I went in. But going home was the best thing that would happen to me for the time being. Home to my own bed and an overwhelming sense of relief. I had plummeted beyond the depths of my comfort zone and was glad to be back in a normal environment.

Did I learn anything from my brief stay in Withington? Yes, I learned how limiting psychiatric care was and how inhumanely I was treated. A bright young woman in distress and left to rot in the corridor of a dirty psychiatric ward by nurses who claimed not to understand me but who never really tried. If they had peeked a little bit harder, broken beyond the veils of my sorrow and distress, they would have seen some truly tumultuous storms looming in the horizon.

TWO

After leaving Withington I tried so hard to get a handle on my life and live a 'normal' existence although that is such a subjective thing. I went back to my teaching job, carried on singing with the choir, but I was very unsettled. I bought my own little property, a quaint mid terraced two bedroomed house which needed a hell of a lot doing to it but was cheap. This became my sanctuary.

Gradually, however, the depression sneaked upon me like a thief in the night and I found myself hospitalised in a slightly more modern hospital in Stockport. It wasn't a hotel, don't get me wrong, but was slightly more hospitable than Withington. We didn't have private rooms back then, unless it was for your own safety. There was a larger room split into 4 separate cubicles, each with a bed and a wardrobe. The really poorly people had a room with their own nurse. Then the less ill you were, the further away from the nurses' station the bed was. I spent quite a few months there, drowning in my sadness. I was very unhappy but it wasn't something I had control over. It wasn't stuff making me depressed. It was something inside my head that I could not navigate. Like something had sucked every bit of happiness from within.

I slept an awful lot. Like most of the day and night. Depression has a way of making you perpetually exhausted. Everything was a humungous effort. Having the will to drag your bones out of bed is something that just doesn't happen. Then there's all the other stuff…showering, bathing, brushing your hair, make-up. None of it seems to matter anymore in the scheme of things. The world becomes a very black place, very heavy, very exhausting. People seem to think you can just make a little more effort, think more brightly, count your blessings. Yeah, like it's that easy, right?

Along with the depression, came the agitation. Frustration too. I would get so irritated and angry with myself. Angry because I seemed to have no control of what was going on inside my head. I had no words to express how I was feeling, I wanted to rip myself to shreds in angst. I would pace around the corridors, jittering and shaking and full of rage and frustration. Desperate for solace. But there was none to be found. I swallowed my pills and prayed for a miracle.

There were some interesting characters who would hang out in the smoke room. Back in the late 90's it was ok to smoke in psychiatric wards. We all hung out in a cloud of smoke, a wired mix of mental afflictions, and tried to socialise. Geoff was an elderly bloke who had been in an accident that had left him with brain damage. He was severely impaired and had no real speech. He communicated in grunts and spent his whole waking time begging for cigarettes. It was a pitiful sight and my heart went out to him. He was harmless enough unless he decided he wanted your cigarette and then he would strike out of desperation, like a praying mantis.

John was a manic depressive who used to be a British Aerospace engineer, but his illness had robbed him of his career. He was very seriously ill and spent a lot of his life in hospital. He had severe depressions and soaring manias. His manias lit up the whole room and he was hilarious and joyous, but it was sobering to see how he lived on the edge every day of his life. John would spend the whole time in the smoking room when he was manic, laughing and joking and being very loud. He became very sexually inappropriate, but it was amusing. You have to laugh at these lighter moments. Life is tragic, but you have to see the funny side.

One day I was mooching in the corridors when I heard a high- pitched scream. There, in a side room, was a youngish woman, bedraggled and covered in perspiration. She moaned and cried in a haunting and terrified manner that pierced through absolutely every other sound. She was distraught and hurled herself around her bed as she screeched. She had just had a new baby and had spiralled into a psychosis as a result of childbirth and motherhood. She was in desperate need of help. Her poor husband and children were devastated, and the girl was suffering very badly indeed. She was gravely ill, mentally, and had an army of nurses and doctors trying their best to bring her out of her psychotic state. She was on the ward many months before she was well enough to return home. She had been a nurse but had to abandon her career. Mental illness does not discriminate. I felt for the woman so terribly.

There was the sweetest little lady called Yvonne who was almost a ghost. She was afraid of everything and everyone and existed in a perpetual state of fear and anxiety. She was a plump lady with unwashed blonde hair who hyperventilated her way through each and every moment. She was so anxious that she was unable to breathe, and her breath came in short, sharp gasps, much like a panting dog. She was on a huge cocktail of anti-anxiety drugs but there seemed to be nothing that the doctors were doing that could help her. She was in so much pain that it was distressing to be around her. She was a cigarette junkie and would smoke one cigarette after another until the nurses put her on a curfew. It had an even more terrible effect as her anxiety quadrupled whilst she was unable to smoke. It was impossible to have a conversation with such an anxious lady as her breath and words came in short sighs and illegible whispers.

By far the biggest influence upon my gullible mind at that time was my meeting with a powerhouse patient named Vanessa. Now Vanessa was a proud Leo, indeed a lioness in her own right. She owned that ward and strutted around like the Queen of England herself. She was a larger girl with a mane of blonde hair. She walked tall and proud and had a larger than life personality. Vanessa, I learned, was manic depressive. Nowadays known as bipolar. She had a fiery disposition and took no prisoners. I would often see her in her volatile moments on the ward, but I liked her a great deal. She was warm and funny. She was also highly intelligent and had been reading English at university when she became ill and had to leave. Mental illness does not discriminate, it claims its customers from all areas of life.

Vanessa's moods were spiralling. She had been treated for a deep depression but had flare ups of rage and fiery aggression. We became firm friends. Looking back, it was perhaps not the most ideal relationship for me at that time, but it was eventful. Vanessa did, however, help me to come out of my depression and for that I am thankful. We would spend many hours in the smoke room laughing and joking and sharing stories. It wasn't ideal. On one occasion we were chilling in the other ward when a woman pushed her luck and said something derogatory to Vanessa who then hurled a cup of hot coffee over the woman and scalded her! Such is life in the psychiatric ward!

After several months on the ward, my depression lifted, and I felt oh so much better. My mind was clear again, thank god and I was no longer agitated and angry and frustrated. My mental capacity had returned, and I was thinking and feeling on top form. I spent a couple of days at home followed by a couple of weeks and was given discharge, to be reviewed at a later date.

I was so delighted to be home. I returned to work, with little embarrassment. Looking back, I never felt any embarrassment or regret. I didn't consider all the upheaval my illness had provoked. I simply got back in the classroom, rolled my sleeves up and got on with life. But all was not as it seemed. My mood seemed to be getting gradually more exuberant as my energy soared and my optimism was unshakable. I started spending nights awake, tapping away at my computer keyboard. I would be cyber surfing into the early hours. I would sing at the top of my voice for hours and hours imagining myself as a famous vocalist or celebrity. I ripped all the carpets up in the house and threw them all out, with grand decorating ideas in mind (that were never fulfilled).

My personal life started spiralling out of control. I was spending a lot of time online in chat rooms, often staying up into the early hours of the morning, then getting up and going to work the next day as fresh as a daisy. It was as though I didn't need any sleep! I started meeting guys I'd picked up through dating agencies and having them back to my house. I was totally oblivious to the risks and as I look back in retrospect, I see how I was playing with fire! I met Julian, who happened to be a charming, VERY handsome professional and he taught me the delights of Tantra. I ceremoniously dumped him shortly after in a moment of boredom as he couldn't keep up with my voracious appetite for pleasure!

I toyed with the quaint idea of becoming a slave in some grotesque S&M bondage situation. I even had the offer to go live in America and have my nipples pierced as part of the package deal. The rest of the deal wasn't so lucrative. I am certain I would have become disillusioned with my ancient, aesthetically challenged Master in about two days and then would have had to commit murder to secure my freedom. However, I don't like blood! Real life just isn't like Fifty Shades of Grey!

Then one night I met David, who would change my life forever. David's internet persona was 'Daithi'. He was an Irish guy from Dublin and 30 years my senior. He was a retired engineer and lived in Abu Dhabi, in the United Arab Emirates, with his partner. He'd previously been married and had two grown up children. David was an alcoholic and a sex addict, but he was a charming man with a dashing smile and sparkling blue eyes. I was smitten. We would meet in a special chat room for hours and hours at all times of day and night. He was a fascinating man but for me in my fragile state he was pure danger. I was playing with fire and I didn't care. My behaviour was becoming more and more risqué and my judgement was deteriorating. I flung myself into a full swing online affair and had no regard for the consequences!

I had become obsessed and immersed in my tempestuous relationship and threw all sense out of the window when David said he was coming over to visit me! I was absolutely over the moon. Bear in mind this guy could have been a serial killer. He could have been a rapist, sadist, psychopath. But my brain was definitely out of kilter. I was so excited and totally oblivious to the risk I was taking! I even offered to leave the door unlocked so he could meet me in my bed! When I look back, alarm bells ring. But I was spiralling upwards at a rate of light years. I fantasised throughout the working day about David's arrival. I even boasted to people at school about my plans! I had no shame, no sense of danger or what was appropriate.

When David arrived, however, he was mild mannered and charming if not rather inebriated! Maybe he was nervous. We clicked immediately. I felt as though I was the lucky one. But what sixty plus guy wouldn't want a young woman half his age hanging off his arm? We wined and dined and then…well use your imagination. Sex was a big thing and he was totally obsessed with it in all its forms. It had played a big part in our online chats previous to our meeting.

When David had to go back to Abu Dhabi after a couple of days it was a huge blow. I adored him and had become obsessed. I would live for the next moment I would see him online. I would sit at the computer all night, desperate to talk to him. My life became consumed by all things David. It was definitely unusual behaviour and should have set warning bells ringing. But back then I had not had a diagnosis so did not recognise the signs.

As my illicit love life ignited my passion, other obsessions came into play. I became a member of a famous Occult Group based in London. This group had various rituals that had to be learned and followed whilst dressed in black robes and brandishing a knife. There were certain grades that were bestowed for knowledge learned and exams successfully completed. It was a noble and honest group, though secretive. Their intentions were honorable, there was nothing dangerous or illegal. Nothing dangerous unless you have a mind that is veered towards psychosis! I became totally obsessed, throwing myself into learning the secrets and rituals. I was convinced I had special magical powers, that I was going to be worshipped and celebrated. I spent hours every day practising and studying. I drove the leader of the group crazy by constantly emailing her and asking questions. I was convinced I was in touch with higher beings in my dreams and that I could make magic and control things with my mind. This all seemed perfectly natural and logical to my racing mind. I was going to be a force to be reckoned with, someone magical and powerful. My bedroom was dark apart from the blazing candles illuminating the blackness. I stood in the middle of the room, ceremonial knife in hand, and chanted the sacred words of the ritual of the Pentagram, a ritual meant for banishing negative forces and also for protection. I would perform the same ritual morning and night, in Hebrew. I would visualise the mighty and powerful archangels, towering above me and granting me their protection. It was very impressive and empowering stuff. I still have a great deal of respect for the work of the occult order. However, my mind was a florid hothouse of grandiose thoughts and aspirations. I was going to be special, hell I was already special. The world would soon know my name! I was going to become such a successful magician. I was going to succeed to the hierarchy and rule the universe!

Besides practising the magical arts and having wild and passionate sexual encounters with the online male population, I was making the most of my freedom and partying hard and wild with former patient

Vanessa, who was also home from hospital. Vanessa made me smile. She was so warm and such fun, especially when you are soaring higher and higher in the grip of a manic phase, although I did not know back then that I was manic. Vanessa had this charming little attribute when she was becoming manic. Food art. Yes! Food art! She would get all the food she could get her hands on and turn it into works of art. Well, she thought they were works of art in her manic state. Mania has the habit of turning the mundane into the fantastical. Something so boring and inane can seem magical and exquisite. In reality, they were just plates of food but to her they were creative genius. And I loved her for it! We were both running fast and hard. I don't think either of us were a hundred percent in control of our rampant desires. We had met a couple of guys in the hospital who had afflictions of their own.

So what better idea than to throw a wild party with our new male pals? The stage was set. A large house with no neighbours. Two young ladies, one of them in the grips of escalating mania and the other one relapsing. A small group of young men, all with mental conditions and recently out of hospital. Seductive music. Piles of alcoholic beverages and the odd joint of weed thrown in. And we're off! It was the craziest, most hedonistic party I'd ever delighted in. The music throbbed, the beer flowed, the laughter exploded and this lady went wild and lost the last inhibitions she ever had. I felt tantalising and special, seductive and alluring. I charmed the guys and chose my victim. I used him for my own personal pleasure then discarded him like a dirty tissue. I was ruthless and insensitive. I had lost all compassion and decency and become a woman with a mission, a self-centred thrill seeker. I ate the guy up and spat him out without a thought for his feelings or embarrassment. I was a heartless bitch, ruthless and out of control.

My euphoric existence was reaching its pinnacle and my unfettered sense of freedom and supreme ecstasy had built an ivory tower around me and my too fast life. But the walls were about to come tumbling down!

THREE

I sat optimistically amongst the assembled nurses and doctors in that stale little interview room at the hospital. The panel of experts eyed me cautiously that fateful morning. It was my review meeting to assess how well I'd been coping since my last admission onto the psychiatric unit. I was a bundle of hyperactivity, of crackling energy reigned in, waiting to be unleashed in all its technicolour glory. I fidgeted on the edge of my seat, my feet tapping and limbs twitching. My eyes shiftily took in every detail of the scene. I was a million miles away from the sad, repressed Sarah of several months ago. Back then I had sat hunched in the corner, eyes averting contact with humankind and speech so slow and subdued. I had been a mere shadow, a non-entity, wishing for anonymity. Where the darkness once had cursed the very depths of my being, bright light illuminated every hidden aspect of my soul.

I did not hold back when questioned about the progress I had made. I blessed the panel of professionals with every intimate detail of the wildness that had been the time of my life. I revealed every sordid indiscretion, revelling in the intense manner with which the doctors were reacting. Every ounce of craziness spewed from my blood red lips and enraptured my captive audience. In my mind I was a heroine, a glamorous film star. My life was alive on the big screen and all the world adored me. Or so I believed.

A stony and exaggerated silence enveloped the room. A sea of concerned faces met my optimistic gaze. If time had stopped, I would still have still heard the ticking of the clock. I faltered slightly as a hint of stale oppression hung in the ether. My expectation did not marry comfortably with the reality as perceived by the group of mental health professionals deciding my fate that day. I remember very clearly who passed the first not so favourable words. My community psychiatric nurse (CPN), I do not remember her name, threw a devastating proverbial blow to the stomach that felt as though I had been given life imprisonment. "We think you need to come back and stay with us," were her simple words. To me, in my wild and manic disposition, she may as well have been offering to gouge my eyes out with a red-hot poker and throw me into a burning pit of hellfire and brimstone for eternity.

I was outraged and insulted. I was as livid as it was possible to be without causing grievous bodily harm to an innocent bystander. I erupted like a volcano that had lay dormant for centuries and finally found its power and majesty. I was a powerhouse of unbridled passion, and anger spewed forth in an unstoppable torrent, destroying all in its meagre path. I shot out of my seat at warp speed and hurled myself out of the door into the corridor. I was a force to be reckoned with, and with my fury came unbelievable physical strength.

As I ran through the corridor my legs felt like sticky treacle. My mind was racing and if I had been relying on mind-power, I would have been on another continent by the time the nurses swung into action. But it was my body I was sadly counting on and although I felt strong and powerful, it was mere seconds before I found myself pinned to the cold, hard concrete floor by a gang of hospital staff. I thrashed and flailed, I punched and kicked and made sure to get in a few juicy bites for good measure. I screamed and shouted the vilest obscenities, bastard this and fucking that. But numbers overcame strength and it was a sorry sight to see this frantic young woman curtailed and controlled in the name of psychiatry.

Well, if they thought this young lady was coming quietly, they had another thing coming. I battled my oppressors like a one-woman army. I fought like a true warrior princess with the tongue of a sailor. I was dragged kicking and screaming into a side room and forced by two male nurses into a painful arm-lock whilst I continued to wreak havoc in my reluctance to cooperate. I refused to calm myself and my screams and raging vocals raised the game to the next level.

A doctor emerged into the room brandishing the biggest needle I had ever witnessed, flanked by an army of nurses. The true horror of the situation dawned on my frantic mind as I was forced onto the bed, face down, restrained and unable to move at all. The wicked needle, my sworn enemy, made its way swiftly to my derriere and with a sharp jab I was rendered unconscious, far away in the land of nothingness and nowhere.

FOUR

Like a modern-day sleeping beauty, I slumbered undisturbed for several days and nights. The carnival of my technicoloured mind had merely settled for a short time. My body was in repose, recouping its strength. I was silent and still, but not lost. I would redeem myself from this imposed nothingness like a phoenix soaring from the ashes. I would rise and conquer.

I awoke within one of the side rooms which were reserved for the acutely ill. I was not alone and now came as a buy one, get one free. I had my own personal nurse in attendance at all times, hampering my style and making me feel like a fraud. Why was I here? I wasn't sick. Never had I felt more alive, in fact. If I could bottle this intense feeling of power and energy throbbing through my mind and body, I would be a multi-millionaire. I heaved myself out of bed and balanced upon shaky, trembling limbs that hadn't seen any action for several redundant days. I tried to piece together exactly what had gone wrong and could vaguely recall the fiery scenario which led to my incarceration.

I had been retained under Section Three of the Mental Health Act. Section Three is a treatment order in the United Kingdom under which the hospital and doctors can treat you as they deem best for your own mental health and recovery. The treatment order is an involuntary admission for a period of up to six months, as deemed appropriate by the psychiatrist. I was a virtual prisoner, at the mercy of the hospital staff. They had deemed me unwell and unable to function in the outside world. According to the establishment, I was a danger to myself and if I wanted to venture back out into the real world, I better accept my treatment and take my medication like a good girl.

So here I was, doing the rounds of the psych ward yet again. Such a glamorous role, that of mental patient. Yet this time was different. This time the doctors weren't trying to lift me back up, they were desperate to bring me down, back within the accepted realms of 'normalcy'. I was flying high, riding the waves of mania on a surfboard of psychosis. As life on the ward hummed along at a generally sedentary rate, I lived in the fast lane, jetting at warp speed into a dazzling culmination. I was an exhausting spectacle in those early days, a whirling dervish of energy. I talked incessantly as I rushed around the corridors, tiring the poor nurses who had to be my companions. For two weeks I was carefully chaperoned, day and night, round the clock. I could not venture off the ward, take a shower in peace, nor even pee in privacy. It was rather degrading, but I was so manic that I really didn't care. I may have been a virtual prisoner, surrendering my sanity into the hands of learned men, but I was having the time of my life! Oh dear mania, bringing joy and sweet insanity. How blessed and yet how cursed.

My spirit was not broken, nor was I allowing myself to be subdued by the hierarchy. The doctor had prescribed a nasty drug called Droperidol, which was an anti-psychotic of choice back in the day. It was the drug from hell. I detested it with venom. It chewed me up and spat me out. As soon as I would swallow it, Armageddon would begin! My mind was racing to infinity, but the terrible drug seemed to slow it down and I just wasn't coping with the internal battleground. I would feel dizzy, my heart would pound like a heavy metal drummer on acid, and I would panic! It really was horrendous. Every morning and every night I would stand at the drug trolley, pleading with the nurses, begging them for mercy. And every day and night I had to endure the same hell. My mind and body were in protest, they had no intention of being subdued!

Drug Trolley

Hail Oh righteous vessel,
Bearer of great gifts to
Those with faith in
This Messiah of psychiatry.
Wondrous drugs
of plentious magnitude,
Neurological , psychological
Sumptuous liquorice allsorts.
Plastering, sanding, glossing
Over crumbling foundations,
Psychological invalidity,
Circuitry overload.
Come now,
Swallow those meds.
They'll send away those voices,
Ease away the pain.
You know you have to cooperate,
For we have needles
Longer than your arm.
Must have complete submission.
Glazed and dazed,
The damaged and cracked,
Assert the tablet hierarchy.
"Only two tonight dear?
I have fifty a day you know".

Blessed consumption of the
Sacred pills and holy water,
Modern deistic ceremony,
After the manner of Sigmund Freud.
As the hoards disperse to
Separate dimensions of space,
Time and delusion,
Broken, shattered fragments
Of a once-whole mirror,
They praise their holy trinity,
In the name of the
Trolley, drug and holy nurse,
AMEN

© *Sarah Drury*

FIVE

One of my passions, shortly before being thrown into the psychiatric ward against my will, was all things Irish. This was influenced heavily by my illicit affair with my dashing Irish pensioner. I had become immersed in the history and culture of Ireland to the extent that I lived and breathed Irish heritage. I bought dozens of CD's of tuneful, nostalgic music sung in the country's mother-tongue. Gaelic. I basked in its beautiful, haunting melodies and enchanting lyrics sung in a language I didn't understand. But my heart understood, and my aesthetic senses were enraptured. The language was beguiling. I poured over texts aimed at teaching the Gaelic language along with the accompanying teach-yourself CD's. I lived and breathed Ireland. The only thing missing was my Irish man, who I yearned for with a broken heart.

I spent hours learning Gaelic. I would let the delightful lingo pour out of my clumsy mouth at a hundred miles an hour, the words colliding in an incoherent jumble. It was a catastrophe in Irish! I had learned a couple of Irish songs too and would have no inhibitions about rendering them at full volume, in the middle of the night! I doubt I was the most popular patient on the ward at that time, but in my manically carefree manner I didn't give a shite! In my mind, I was a supremely talented being, a superstar, destined for fame and fortune. Who wouldn't want to hear me?

Some nights I would sit on the bed trying hard to concentrate on the TV whilst my every movement was being monitored by a nurse. I had the attention span of a goldfish. One of the nurses, a half Indian guy, said something that to this day really hurts me. He actually said "Sarah, you know people like you should never have children?". Honest to goodness, those were his words!!! In this modern age of political correctness, he would never be allowed to say something like that. It is simply unethical and very judgemental. If a nurse said that today, there would be outrage! At the time he said it, I was not in my best state of mind, so took no further action. Looking at it now, I am incensed. Mental illness poses challenges, but there must be millions of mothers and fathers in my situation. To hear such downright prejudice coming out of the mouth of a mental health nurse is preposterous and quite shocking. I didn't heed his warning as I did eventually become a mother, but more of that later.

As the dust gradually settled and I stopped screaming at the nurses and hurling my dinner across the room, I was allowed small privileges. The nights were sleepless and never ending. I was penniless with no smokes. There were two very kind nurses who treated me with respect and compassion. Colin was a handsome young guy, with sandy hair and John Lennon spectacles, who cut a dashing figure. He was charming with a superb sense of humour and a real pleasure to be around. As well as being easy on the eye, he had a real kindness about him. He was calm and well-mannered and always had a dashing smile for me. The nights were long and sleepless, and my tiny room was suffocating. Colin would let me sit with him in the patients' TV room in the dead of night. There was stillness all around and not even a mouse dared sneeze. My mind was racy, and my tongue was fast. I found humour in the mundane and my mouth had no inhibitions. When I had been sectioned, my rights as a citizen had been pretty much curtailed. I had no access to my money (though that was not a bad thing) so had no secret stashes of smokes or chocolate. I was under lock and key with no way to sustain my cigarette habit. I was at the mercy of whichever saviour selflessly offered me a smoke. Colin was my saviour on those endless manic nights. He smoked roll ups which seemed anorexic compared to the full-fat Benson & Hedges I usually puffed. It was quite a surprise putting Colin's roll up in my mouth that first time. It was small and thin and emaciated. I remember laughing and telling him, shamelessly, it felt like giving a pencil a blow job! He must've been amused by my runaway mouth as my words were all over the ward the next day!

Another nurse who showed me a great deal of kindness during that difficult time was a wonderful lady named Jill. She was such a kind soul yet had such an outgoing personality. She was a bundle of joy! When I was at my worst, swearing and cursing and throwing my dinner or my medication at unsuspecting nurses, she never treated me with anger or resentment. I know that would be unprofessional now but back then, it was pretty much a national lottery! She treated me with respect and laughed with me, never ridiculing my behaviour. I am forever grateful to her for helping me through my wilder manic days.

My mania was proving expansive. Although being on a psychiatric ward would be any average person's worst nightmare, I was having rather a lovely time. Let's face it, when you're caught up in the fires of mania, everything pulsates with excitement. Life is grandiose, like the silver screen, and everyone's a hero. I was consumed by sexual energy and even being a porn queen seemed like a very agreeable proposition. Thankfully I didn't actually turn to the porn industry, but I did become rather fond of cherry red lipstick and a faux fur coat. I treasured that jacket. I felt like a movie star when I stalked the corridors stark naked but for the fur coat draped around my nubile form. I would prowl the ward, biding my time, red lips lush and pouting, waiting for my victim. As an unsuspecting male appeared, I would strike. I would pull open my coat and reveal my shameless body in all its youthful glory. To see the look of shock on people's faces was priceless! The thrill was immense but soon scuppered by the spoilsport nurse ushering me back to my room to 'put myself away'. I'm surprised the ward's male visiting figures didn't quadruple! They could have charged admission and made a few quid on the side for a staff night out!

The exhibitionist in me didn't stop there. I would spend many hours sitting in the smoking room with fellow patients. There was this shy and subdued nursing assistant, I forget his name. He was a mole-like fellow with thick, black hair, strong brows and round spectacles framing short-sighted eyes. He never spoke much and almost never laughed. He reminded me of the character Adrian Mole. He would supervise us unruly types with hardly a word, making observations whilst hunched over a clipboard, pen scribbling away intermittently. I decided that I would give this quiet fellow the shock of his life! The moment he looked up from his clipboard, I threw my blouse over my head, and not having the support of a bra that day, the poor guy was treated to a full frontal! Well, his face! He almost died, he blushed the colour of a tomato at its ripest and started blustering and stuttering. I found this hysterical! He

rushed out of the room at lightning speed in a state of what probably was extreme embarrassment. Looking back, I still find
it funny though in a school-girl kind of way! I would love to see what his clipboard had to say about that!

I had been a soprano singer with the Halle Choir in Manchester for several years, and had sung all my life. My mother's mother was a cabaret singer and my father's mother was a piano teacher, so music was in my blood. Being manic exaggerated this a thousand times! I was told that I sang for three days and nights without stopping when I first came onto the ward. There was this charming patient who reminded me very much of Bette Davis's character in the film 'Whatever Happened to Baby Jane'. She was an ample lady with long, frizzy, white hair, quite unkempt. She must have been about seventy years old, either that or she hadn't aged well and wasn't blessed with a youthful complexion. She was a manic-depressive patient in the throes of a spiralling mania and extremely exuberant and vocal. She had been a professional singer in her heyday and, like myself, wasn't shy about belting out the odd song. I was just happy to sing, whilst she desperately craved an audience. I don't know how she found out I could hold a tune, but before I knew it I had been lured into a duet. My specialism at the time was Pie Jesu by Andrew Lloyd Webber. I must admit it sounded beautiful. I did have the voice of angel back then. Sadly, I have the vocals of an asthmatic docker nowadays. Before I knew it, I had been enlisted as this lady's choral partner in crime. We used to sit happily outside the main ward entrance, for hours at a time, baring our souls through song. Imagine, two manic ladies imagining they were on the stage of the Royal Albert Hall! We probably sounded more like cats wailing in the alley!

Being on a psychiatric ward, you meet people from all walks of life. Each patient has their own story. Every illness affects people in different ways. I had, up until now, been diagnosed with depression although had had symptoms of a mood disorder. But now I was given the diagnosis of manic depression, known nowadays as bipolar disorder. I was treated with a terrible antipsychotic called Droperidol, which had dreadful side effects. I have been on all kinds of pills in my search for mental relief. Most of them didn't work or worked for a while. Medication is trial and error. Having a mental illness requires a great deal of courage, regardless of how many meds you take.

There was one girl on the ward who my heart goes out to. She was a tiny scrap of a girl, barely noticeable. She was small and emaciated with wispy blonde hair and sallow skin. Her eyes were insipid, a pale blue, and sunk into dark sockets. She looked as though she had never had a decent meal in her life and her movements were twitchy and unpredictable. She was like a shadow, afraid to be seen in the light of day. She spoke in muted, breathy whispers and each word was a cry for help. She had a very damaged childhood with a terrible history of abuse and neglect. It had left her broken and needy. She craved love and attention. Her every act was a desperate plea but relief was never found. She had thrown herself off the motorway bridge in sheer desperation. She sustained terrible injuries, multiple fractures, and it was a miracle she had not lost her life. I do not know if it had been a plea for help or a genuine suicide attempt, but she must have been in so much pain, emotionally. She was in a wheelchair on the ward, with a nurse. Her doting husband, who cared for her night and day, never left her side. He was devastated but showed only love and devotion to his angel. She was a complex character. Such was her pain, that she craved companionship day and night. Maybe she just didn't feel safe in her own company, maybe she was filled with frustration and self-loathing. I could never begin to understand her torment, but I hope she one day found peace with herself.

Another interesting character I became friends with was Julia, a girl in her early twenties who had been diagnosed with paranoid schizophrenia. Julia was a pleasant, easy going girl who was having big problems with delusions. She was convinced that there was a huge conspiracy and that her real father was Elvis Presley. She would talk for hours about Elvis in a rambling, disorganised way that would confuse the listener but made perfect sense to her. She knew all the intricate secrets of Gracelands and of her famous family in America. Delusions are false ideas. Thoughts that can't possibly be true. Like thinking your mother is really Pope Francis or that your father is Beyonce. I had never encountered anyone with delusions before, so I found the whole situation quite difficult to understand. I was later to have delusions of my own, but back then I didn't have so much empathy. We all have coping mechanisms, and mine was to act as though everything was perfectly ordinary even though deep down it all confused the hell out of me. So, whenever Julia would tell me her stories of her celebrity parentage I would smile and listen and nod my head politely. Manners hurt no one, especially not in a psychiatric hospital! Besides, it was far more interesting than the telly!

One of my buddies on the ward was a young lad called Paul. He couldn't have been older than twenty. Paul had some fascinating delusions and hallucinations that kept him on cloud nine for hours on end! He would journey into other dimensions of time and space. His adventures were incredible, and he would tell me wonderful tales of new galaxies he'd seen in glorious technicolour! He was an excitable bloke, wildly animated and joyous. He had schizophrenia and at times his speech was disorganised and chaotic, but I could have listened to his tales of space travel for hours and I would happily have been his assistant, just like Doctor Who!

'Chill Pill'

Hail! Oh, hallowed Saviour
Of society!
This crazy epidemic of insanity,
Life between the veils,
What's real, what's fantasy?
Clutching, clawing, grasping at reality,
Go chill, take a pill, the sane mill,
Travesty,
It's uncool, madness, such an insane
Malady,
Yet grounding, rooting, back to body
Gravity,
Miracles of modern medics
Clarity,
So, take it, just a pill, for total
Equinamity.

© Sarah Drury

SIX

I had moved to Manchester when I was nineteen, to study at the Manchester Metropolitan University. I had studied for a Bachelor of Education degree specialising in music. University had been a blast. Great friends, good times, worked hard, played harder. I never had any signs of depression back then. If anything, I was slightly wild and leant towards the manic side of things. I was bright and gregarious, confident and positive. I had good friends and a fabulous social life. I was always engaged in a myriad of hobbies and activities. Life was wonderful.

I graduated with a good degree and blagged my way into a fantastic job in one of Manchester's better schools. I continued to live life in the fast lane, juggling a stressful teaching career with wild nights of music and drink and wonderful cuisine. I was a soprano in a famous choir which took me all over Europe, performing with some of the biggest names in classical music. I was a success story on all accounts. My family were so proud of me. My mother made the journey to hear me perform whenever she could. I performed at the Proms in the Royal Albert Hall, I sang for the Queen, I sang with Bjork (the popular singer) and two of the Three Tenors. I couldn't have wished for a better, more successful life.

So, to find myself, the family golden girl, locked away from my fabulousness made me feel like a washed-up celebrity. There was no paparazzi, no applause and zero adulation. Home was a modern-day asylum and life became surreal. Mania has the ability to turn mundane into spectacular. Bland becomes vivid, and monochrome, technicolour. It was like drifting off to sleep on a feather-lined pillow, then waking up on a bed of nails. I felt like Alice in wonderland, falling into a land of strange curiosities without the delights, where every person I met was 'curiouser and curiouser'. The engine was on warp speed and I was on a collision course with insanity.

It is rather a shock to find oneself at the mercy of the doctors. I was a teacher, I had my queendom where I called the shots, but was banished to a strange land, of sensible bedtimes and character-building therapies. A land where mind altering psychiatric drugs were a reality, not an option. A land of limitation and oppression.

There was a loose routine which gave a sense of structure to a place where time was not for the patients. Time is immaterial in a psychiatric hospital. Irrespective of what time it was, I knew I was insane for the rest of my life. Medication was doled out at ten in the morning and ten at night. The ward sister would wheel out this huge, metal, maximum-security 'drug trolley'. No-one had access to the trolley except for the nurse in charge of that shift. The wheels of the trolley squeaked like a mouse being mauled by a predator, as they trundled along the corridor. "Meds time!" the nurse would shout and slowly the patients would meander, zombie-like, and take their place in the queue of medicinal compliance. There were potions and pills of a myriad of hues. Promises to fix the broken minds and souls of the poorly people. Back then, medication options were less extensive than they are today. The old antipsychotics like droperidol and haloperidol had some horrendous side effects. I was force-fed the former and the effect was unbearable. I would create dramatic scenes with the nurses until one day I no longer had to take the vile poison! I had been diagnosed with bipolar disorder although back then it was known as manic-depression. It explained a lot! Like how I was travelling at the speed of light in the centre of my own solar system. I was the star of my show and didn't want to relinquish my lead role as a success story, to star as 'newly diagnosed bipolar girl'.

Mealtimes provided some relief from the daily tedium. In the beginning, I had a nasty habit of shouting obscenities, and hurling my dinner at the nursing staff, so was forced to eat in my little private cell. Eventually I showed more restraint and my wilder urges were curtailed, so I was trusted with metal knives and forks in the dining hall, with the other patients. It was surprisingly civilised! The food was edible and let's face it, had to be better than trying to cook when you're either a) drugged up to the eyeballs, b) too manic to be trusted with cooking apparatus or c) just plain idle.

In an attempt at rehabilitation, occupational therapy was introduced into hospitals. In the old asylums, patients were virtual prisoners, twenty-four hours a day, with nothing to take their shattered minds away from the tedium and nothingness. They lived their lives hopelessly, in despair. Their days were endless and mundane. They wandered around aimlessly like mindless sheep and had no direction. Occupational therapy was introduced to bring a sense of purpose to life in an institution and to promote new skills which could be productive. O.T.

also helped to develop confidence and improve concentration and focus. On offer at Stepping Hill, where I was whiling away my days, were the delights of woodwork or pottery. As I have trouble even so much as knocking a nail into a piece of wood, I opted for the latter. Twice a week I would get off the ward, set free amidst the slabs of wet clay, with unlimited potential. I would revel in the slippery substance, slick with water, squishing between my fingers. It was therapy at its finest. The good thing about occupational therapy is that there's no pressure. Nobody has any expectations of you. You do not have to be the next Rodin or Picasso. You are playing with wet clay in a mental hospital, not creating the next exhibit for the Tate Gallery. I happened to adore the slickness of the smooth clay, to palpate its soggy substance. It became a true form of release after the tedium that was daily psychiatric living.

As time passed, it became obvious that recovery was going to take quite some time. The soaring heights of my mania did reach more manageable levels, but the simmering hypomania remained. I was still as excitable as a clinical chocoholic with a VIP pass to Willy Wonka's chocolate factory. I wasn't exhausting all who endured me with grandiose flights of fancy, and dreams of fame and fortune, but something disturbed was bubbling beneath the surface, something restless and child-like. The many months of tedious regime had created a perturbed ghoul, a claustrophobic spirit of rebellion and anarchy. A soul who wanted her first taste of freedom.

How does a highly excitable psychiatric patient on a six-month statement, with no money, no leave of absence and absolutely no means of transport make a great escape? Sounds impossible doesn't it? I managed to get my twitchy hands on my bank card by some unscrupulous methodology and as it was my passport to the outside world, kept it safe from prying eyes like a taboo secret. I was unable to leave the ward due to previous attempts at breaking free, so I sat incognito by the main entrance doors to the ward. I sat. I sat some more. I sat all morning. Then holy Mary Mother of God herself showered me with her blessings and I was out of those doors faster than an Olympic champion. Though with far less finesse and absolutely zero strategy. I sailed through the corridors, the wind whistling beneath my feet. I hopped on the local bus and hitched a lift to the train station. The station was a busy and confusing place, noisy and fast paced, heaving with people of all shapes, sizes and orientations. I was somewhat overwhelmed by the open space and lack of direction, but I jumped the train to Scunthorpe and spent the whole of the journey concealed in the toilet! It was the smelliest, most cramped and unpleasant two hours I had ever spent, but certainly the most exciting! I was free! Away from the confines of the institution at long last! I was alive, kicking and living on the edge of danger! I must've called my mother as when I arrived at Scunthorpe station, my whole family rejoiced as they welcomed me on the platform. There was an expectant buzz in the air that day I gloriously, shamelessly, rebelled against the establishment.

The police came hammering at the door that evening. They had come to inform my mother that her daughter was officially a missing person. My mother fears no-one and laughed in the faces of officialdom. She was honest and confessed the fact that I was sleeping sweetly beneath a plump, luxurious duvet. I was terrified that the officers would cart me back to that godforsaken hole, but an arrangement was reached giving me a few more days' freedom to bask in the soothing waters of my loving family.

SEVEN

I was fresh out of hospital and although I was no longer manic, I was still impulse-driven and reckless. My infatuation with the Irish engineer was totally consuming my life. I had left my teaching job and spent my days pining like a love-sick and celebrity-infatuated teenager. I had flown out to the Emirates for an illicit holiday and left with a huge yearning for all things Arabian. My life seemed stagnant and meaningless, empty and aimless. I wanted just to soar high above my problems and follow my passions, wherever they would take me.

Then an inspirational idea pierced my awareness. Bingo! Why didn't I go and get a teaching job in the Emirates? Just the thing to do when you've had to leave your previous teaching position due to being diagnosed with a severe mental illness! Run away from your home, your family, your friends, your whole support network! I scoured the web looking for teaching jobs in Abu Dhabi and within a week I was packing my suitcase.

As I boarded the plane to the emirates, my whole soul was buzzing. I was in hyper drive mode! I had lost my senses and merely abandoned my life in Manchester. Literally. I'd packed a suitcase, locked my door and turned my back on the last twelve devastating months. I had no psychiatrist, only a few weeks of medication and no work visa. I boarded that plane like an immigrant, seeking a miracle in a land of golden opportunity. I was in complete denial that I had a serious mental illness and was moving to a country where such illness is the work of the devil.

I stood at the top steps of the aircraft to be blasted by a wall of heat. This place was hot! Abu Dhabi is part of the United Arab Emirates, a land of camels marching through sand dunes, silhouetted against blazing sunsets. The city of Abu Dhabi is an Island in the Persian Gulf. It is ultra-modern with incredible architecture, beautiful modern structures, many of them with a traditional Arabian twist. The futuristic buildings soared upwards, penetrating the stratosphere, like escalators to the gates of some twenty-first century kingdom of heaven. There were residential areas, ranging from stunning apartment blocks bedecked with balconies and bougainvillea, to concrete huts with no running water or electricity for the poor Pakistani taxi drivers. Some of the poorer immigrants didn't even have a home and would sleep beneath the palm trees. There were many leisure facilities, though only the wealthier immigrants had access to them. The streets were lined with palm trees which made it feel like you were living the dream on an L.A. film set! Millions of pounds had been spent irrigating this garden paradise and it was a miracle to see such a green oasis in a desert land! Water was a precious commodity and celebrated by beautifully designed fountains, dotted around the city. Basically, I felt like I'd flown to heaven on a winged Prozac. I had a new life now, a fresh start, and nobody knew the troubles I'd seen.

I was escorted to my apartment in the Khalidya district. I had expected, being a western expatriate, swanky modern accommodation in a desirable part of town. Imagine my surprise when my home for the next two years was in a scruffy, elderly building complete with huge red cockroaches congregating on the doorstep in the evenings, having their little insect parties. I was sharing the top floor apartment with a lovely lady, who had infinite amounts of patience and kindness. The apartment was huge, with a balcony and views of the mosque next door. The mosque was eerily quiet except for Fridays, when the pavement would become a sea for the wave of devout Muslims giving thanks and praise to Allah. It was extraordinary to see such mass devotion, especially from poor immigrant workers who sacrificed their homes and families back in their native countries to work like slaves for a mere pittance and atrocious living conditions.

The school was a beautiful place to work. The staff were uplifting and supportive, from a wide range of backgrounds. The last environment I had worked in had meant having a thick skin. There had been a lot of bitchiness and double dealing and I had made an exhibition of myself in the wild way I had behaved due to my mania. This was a fresh start, however, not only from a work point of view, but from the fact that no one here knew about my psychiatric history. I had a small class of eighteen young children who were all Arabic but spoke fluent English. I loved the children and they were very affectionate and extremely well behaved. I managed to show up for work every day, although it wouldn't be long before the ghosts of my past insanity would start to haunt me.

It was something so simple that burst the fragile bubble of a secure psyche. In the kitchen of the old apartment was a gas cooker. Now, in Abu Dhabi there is no mains gas supply. It is supplied by tall gas canisters that attach to the cooker with a rubber pipe and a valve. This didn't seem to bother anyone else, but I became fixated and absolutely convinced that the gas canister would explode in a blazing inferno. I would turn the valve off constantly, which interfered with the gas supply. This unease progressed to a full-blown psychosis as throughout the city streets there were gas canisters outside shops and apartments. I became very disturbed to the point I was terrified to go out into the street. I would cross the road just to avoid the imagined danger of an exploding canister and as they were everywhere, just being outside became a trauma of epic proportions. I realised that maybe I needed to seek professional help, so found a private hospital with a bored looking, Indian psychiatrist. I booked an appointment and within an hour was clutching a prescription for olanzapine, an antipsychotic. At that time, I was paying for my prescriptions and the cost of my Depakote and the Olanzapine set me back about five hundred dirhams, which at that time was roughly a hundred pounds a month, a tenth of my monthly salary.

I took the Olanzapine religiously, praying for it to be the holy miracle that banished the demons of my psychosis. I would sit in the doctor's office once a month, as he listened with disinterest and heard the pound signs kerch-ing. He had little to offer except a hole in my purse where my dirhams used to be. Then I came upon the psychiatric hospital in Abu Dhabi, and the wonderful Dr Lloyd. Dr Lloyd was a dashing, highly educated Arab, who had trained and worked in London and was the resident psychiatrist at the hospital. The hospital itself was a majestic, pink paradise, the Buckingham Palace of psychiatric institutions. The stunning architecture was a tonic, but it was a million miles away from the putrid hell holes I had endured in the UK. The interior of the hospital was eerily silent. There were no thrashing, desperate patients battling their demons, nor sobbing, hysterical wrecks pleading for sanity. The corridors were empty, like an old abandoned asylum, but of this modern era.

Mental illness in the U.A.E at that time was somewhat taboo. It was a shameful thing to have a mental illness and psychiatry and psychology as practices were not well understood or well regarded. In the U.A.E., there is so much stigma and superstition surrounding mental illness that for many years it has prevented sick people getting the treatment they so desperately need. Widespread beliefs that such illness is a result of poor religious faith and devotion puts a shameful slant on the whole idea of psychiatric treatment or psychological therapy. It was also thought that mental illness could be some kind of curse, by the power of the evil eye. Such restricting beliefs can be found even today. The families of the afflicted would turn to faith healers or religious people to try and restore the patient's weak faith or cast asunder the treacherous evil spirits trapped within. Gradually, attitudes are changing and there is more access to healthcare, but such stigma will take a very long time to overcome. For an ex-patriate like me, drowning in psychosis amidst a stigmatised people, this spanking new hospital was an absolute life saver. As I had a health card, I got my consultation for free, from a highly trained shrink, with no waiting times! And rather than fork out such a fortune for terribly overpriced pills, I got them for five pounds a month! Absolute bargain!

The psychosis never did really go away. I always lived in fear and trepidation of the dreaded gas canisters which were perpetually conspiring to explode in my presence! I was so disturbed that I was forced to move into an all-electric apartment. I managed to live a relatively normal day-to-day life, though I am rather certain my employers realised there was more than meets the eye, and that I had some mental health issues. I was becoming a master of deception, veiling my unsettled thoughts and emotions and putting on a fragile mask. The bright sunshine had a very positive effect on my affect, as during the two years I stayed in Abu Dhabi, not once did my mood plummet. There were no days wallowing in choking blackness. The sun was a natural antidepressant, flooding every atom of my being with a feeling of positivity and energy.

I managed to stay in the U.A.E. for two happy years and even though psychosis plagued my days, I was able to overcome it, with the help of medication, a good psychiatrist and plenty of courage and determination. I enjoyed some of the finest days of my life in that city of blazing heat, crystal blue seas, impeccable cuisine and consumerism to die for. Had my psychosis blossomed into a full blown mania, however, maybe I would have seen how it is to be an inpatient on a shiny new psychiatric unit in the land of mental health stigma!

EIGHT

Whilst life in Abu Dhabi had been one long blast of sun, sea, sand and psychosis, I wasn't quite prepared for the return to my hometown. I had sold my little house in Stockport for a measly sum and moved in with my mother, in a sleepy Lincolnshire village. My mother is the most giving, generous and angelic of beings. She has made sacrifices all her life and is the Mother Theresa of matriarchs. She would give her last pound to the needy and has this wonderful quality of treating every person with compassion and without prejudice. I love my mother dearly. Three husbands later, she has risen from the ashes of her marriages like a phoenix reborn, strong, feisty and totally independent.

Keadby is a world apart from the glamorous U.A.E. Set beside the River Trent, there is nothing particularly noteworthy about the village, except for its fairly old bridge and canal. With a population of about two thousand people, it has some local amenities such as a primary school and a couple of shops. Daily life back home was fairly humdrum. I had my mother and two sisters around me and we shared some happy times for a while. We would go shopping and spend raucous nights at the local karaoke. I could still belt out a tune back then, and started to make new friends who shared my love of music. I had no binding responsibilities, no little people in need of their mummy's devoted attention. No extortionate mortgage to pay, no bills, no crushing debts. I was as free as a soaring Eagle, yet I didn't appreciate my life of luxury. I was contributing to the household in a financial sense but lived an unfettered existence.

I was unreputably content for a while, then slowly the corners of my joyful smile began to slide downwards, as subtle shades of grey dampened the gentle gaiety. Stillness started to lure me from my busyness. At first it was a weariness, dragging me down, energy seeping out of my slowing body with every passing minute. I wished just to sleep, to turn my face away from the light and bury my saddening soul beneath a duvet grave. The joyful days became dragging, endless, joyless. Daylight was my enemy and I retreated from the day like a fearful creature of the shadows. Sleep became my refuge. The hours of the ticking clock ceased to discriminate, and each hour chimed perpetual midnight. I dragged my excuse of a body around like a dead weight, not wanting to move from the warm spot between my bedsheets. The most pleasurable things in life became bleak and thankless. I stopped making an effort with my appearance, looking more like a bag lady with every passing day. Pyjamas became my new dress code, the haute couture of the deeply depressed. Days trickled into weeks as I sank lower and lower into an ocean of darkness and despair. My family were becoming concerned. I looked like a train wreck and felt ten times worse, mentally. The past three years of fast living had finally taken their toll. I was paying the price. And boy was it extortionate!

I had become involved with the local mental health services in Lincolnshire when I returned from living in Abu Dhabi. I had a social worker, a lovely Indian lady, who would visit me regularly at my parents' home. It was suggested I see the psychiatrist who was not happy with my progress. I was deeply depressed and really did not care where I was or what I was doing so long as it didn't take any effort on my part. The world around me could be swept up in Armageddon and I wouldn't have cared less. So when the doctor recommended I go onto the psychiatric ward for treatment, I unenthusiastically cooperated. As long as it didn't involve making an effort to be mentally present, I was fine with that. I packed my bag with a few measly belongings and checked myself onto the ward.

Now my stays on Ward Eighteen are just faded memories in my mind, perhaps because the depression is more difficult to remember or maybe due to the fact that I had my brain blasted to smithereens with Electro Convulsive Therapy. But I shall try my best to recall this dark and unfavourable part of my life. Ward Eighteen was a mental health unit within a hospital. It was an old, dirty, shabby building with several dormitories (single sex of course), a few single rooms for the acutely ill and the usual therapy and meeting rooms. There was a large patient's lounge which allowed smoking. Downstairs there was a dining room and a large recreation room. Life on the ward was very claustrophobic. There was a total lack of privacy and nowhere to escape the stresses of life on a psychiatric unit. Like living inside a giant pressure cooker. It is insane that being hospitalised on a psychiatric ward should be a time of refuge and peace, a place to get away from the trauma and stress of mental illness, a time for recuperation and rehabilitation. Yet it is far from that! Not only are you tearing your soul apart dealing with your own mental illness and anxieties, but you are often surrounded by people who are acutely disturbed. The stress is unbelievable and can make things much worse. Ward Eighteen was a place where there was nowhere to go to escape insanity. It was a huge stew of mental illnesses, all bubbling together in the same psychological boiling pot.

My bed was in a dormitory with other women. Opposite me was a young girl who was desperately fighting a battle with anorexia. She was terrifyingly skeletal and refusing to let a mere morsel of food pass her parched lips. She was on intravenous fluids but was physically and mentally broken. I would try so hard not to overhear as her parents pleaded with her to take even a tiny mouthful. They were so desperate. It was pitiful and heart-breaking. The poor girl was a young teenager, she should have been having fun with her friends at the movies, lusting after boyfirends, going to crazy parties and making the most of her carefree youth. Instead she was a prisoner of her mind, the jail-keeper and tormentor of her broken body. There were other people I met during that stay but they all paled into insignificance. The girl with anorexia saddened me so much that I will always hold a prayer for her in my heart.

Ward Eighteen was not the most enriching environment for my depressive state. I would either lie comatose in my bed, wishing for death to come and release me from the uninspiring throes of life, or while away the hours in the day lounge, smoking myself to an early grave, my charred fingers clutching at the burnt dock-ends, yellow and stinking. The day lounge was everything you see on films of the era depicting mental institutions. It was a big, smoggy room with chairs scattered around its perimeter and dirty, smoke-stained windows looking out onto the real world. The patients were an eclectic mix of characters, some heavily medicated, some wildly manic. It is not good to stereotype, but when you have spent time in a psychiatric institution, sometimes you find yourself playing a personal game of 'what's the disorder'! There will be the desperately depressed, with wrists cut to shreds and a look of death, with a heartbeat; the manic person who is spinning wild stories of their plans to overthrow the queen's empire. Then there's the manic depressive who has become grandiose and psychotic and thinks they're Jesus's third incarnation, complete with the heavenly host of seraphim and cherubim! The schizophrenic, the borderline personality and so on. And do you know what? I don't care what your disorder is, you have my utmost respect if you're struggling day to day with a mental health problem. Hell on Earth!

There is never any decent TV in all the psychiatric wards I have been on! None of the Sky Channels work. And even if there were, I doubt the patients would be able to agree on what to watch. I didn't watch TV as my poor, sad brain could not hold a decent memory for even a minute. I would sit in my saggy, faux leather chair, my brain a quagmire of psychiatric stew, contemplating death as though it were a coveted trophy. I was an actress in this bizarre psychological drama and my role was suicide.

I remember being so physically and mentally wrung out that I wanted to cease living. I would have preferred to have faded away like a bad memory rather taken my own life. I wasn't a pro-active suicide risk despite undisputedly wishing for death. I wanted to be dead, but I didn't want to kill myself. A conundrum of peculiar dimensions? I think what I wanted above all else was HELP! I think this is the case for many people suffering with depression, especially young people. There is suicide and my heart goes out to all those who have been touched in this way, patients and families alone, and then there is a cry for help. The longer I was on the ward, the more issues surfaced. Agitation became an issue. This huge degree of pressure would build within me and I would feel like a mighty explosion was about to rock my inner equilibrium. I would pace desperately around the corridors, pent up angst within my mind, pleading with the nurses to help me. I would beg for thioridazine, an anti-psychotic, which would take the edge off my unease.

The psychosis was a living nightmare. Paranoid delusions, which even led the specialists to question whether I had schizophrenia. Everywhere I went, people were watching me, following me, stalking me. Not only that, but they were putting thoughts into my head! I was no longer in control of my own cognitive processes! People were controlling my mind, telling me to harm myself, to burn myself, to cut myself. The mental pain was horrendous! I became violent and aggressive, frustrated and threatened. I would hide myself away like a recluse and plot ways in which to harm myself. It was a pain so desperate, so bitter that all I thought about was creating a perfect finale. Sweet suicide.

Not only was I hearing voices, but I was in a constant state of fear due to other aspects of the psychosis. I could perpetually smell burning and even see smoke and this kept me on the edge of terror. Hearing voices, delusions, hallucinations are not really the icing on the cake when the sponge itself is depression. Evil faces would appear before me, taunting and mocking and scaring the shit out of me. Hypnotic, terrifying eyes would peer out from the mirror. I was convinced I was the victim of a demonic possession.

The doctors recommended a course of ECT, known as electro-convulsive therapy. I had sixteen sessions of this treatment and it wasn't for the faint hearted. When my great grandmother was in an old asylum, ECT was a very different beast. It was barbaric, the treatment being administered without muscle relaxants or anaesthetic. Things are very different nowadays. It's a very simple affair. A small anaesthetic is administered, with a muscle relaxant to protect against bodily damage during the convulsion, then the two electrodes are applied to the temples and a short shock zaps your sorry, depressed brain. Your body then convulses for about half a minute and you wake up with one hell of a headache and a bit of memory loss as an added bonus. It works for some and not for others. For myself it was a miracle, for it gave me my sanity and thus my life back for a short while.

NINE

I was now in my thirty-fifth year and since my last admission to ward eighteen. My life seemed more settled. I had purchased my own property, a humble, two bedroomed, terraced house, in what could be called the ghetto of Scunthorpe. The house was quite a pleasant little haven amidst an environment where prostitution, drug addiction and gang fights were a normal part of everyday life. The house was conveniently located for the town centre and also for the local club where I would while away many an evening with my musical friends, commanding the microphone as I belted out such classics as Eva Cassidy and Shania Twain.

The area knew much poverty. There was a chemist across the road which used to dispense methadone to the drug addicts. They would form an orderly queue at the back door, some emaciated and bedraggled, skeletal and jittery. They would be forced to swallow their methadone under the chemist's watchful gaze. Methadone is a desirable substance on the black market, and is often traded for hard cash. Drugs were a big problem in this part of town. They were the fountain of criminal activity born out of desperation. The area was a crime hotspot. From these desperate souls' dependency emanated a burning need for the means to satisfy their overpowering urges, and the method of doing so would often lead to criminality. Burglary, such a terrible crime for its victims who feel violated and disturbed, is often fuelled by drugs. Mugging, even in broad daylight is another, even more sickening when it is a vulnerable, elderly person as the victim. There would occasionally be fights between different cultures. These could turn nasty with frightening consequences. Knives could be involved and there were a couple of violent stabbings during my time in the locality.

Some of the more interesting but indeed very sad aspects of life here were the ladies of the night. Often addicts themselves and frail and meagre in body, these women would hang around the street corners a few streets away, plying for trade. They would sell their bodies and indeed their souls for their next hit of heroin or crack. Putting themselves in grave danger, they would lure potential customers, seedy men cruising at walking pace in their cars, throwing themselves open to all kinds of abuse. In fact, laying their lives on the line, though not in a heroic manner! The sad thing is that as addicts, their lives probably don't mean much to most people. For a woman to sacrifice her body to men who will use her and toss her aside like a used condom, for a substance which will undoubtedly be her death sentence, is heart breaking.

Walking the dog in the local park was like dicing with death. The space was a favourite hangout for the lost and lonely, especially the inebriated alcoholics, nursing their bottles of cheap cider and cans of Special Brew as though they were the last precious drops of alcohol on the planet. They would hunch together, sprawled on the warped wooden benches, shouting obscenities and filth to all and sundry. They may have been intimidating but they were quite harmless as they were probably too pissed to stand up and cause any kerfuffle. Littered around the benches were hypodermic syringes, the tools of the trade for the heroin addicts. These were quite alarming as there were often innocent children around, who would think nothing of handling them out of curiosity. These mingled in with the spent beer cans, to create a hot bed of addicts' cast offs.

My neighbours were rather troublesome. They were a couple in their twenties, but due to extensive drug abuse, they were both frail and emaciated and neither had any teeth. Their complexions were patchy and pale, and their skin littered with pock marks and unsightly blemishes. They both looked twenty years older than they actually were. The woman worked as a prostitute on the local streets, her partner being her pimp. They seemed pleasant at first, polite and cordial, but the situation soon became a nightmare of epic proportions. They would scream at each other day and night, a torrent of vile profanity, at a volume that would rock the foundations of the house. Walls were no protection from the cacophony and it became tiresome and intrusive. They would knock on the door begging for money and food and if we refused they would hurl verbal abuse at us. One morning they shoved scraps of food through our letterbox. The woman had a huge fall out with her partner and begged me to stay on the sofa for the night. Eventually they were evicted, and both went to prison for theft, prostitution and assorted dabbles with the criminal underworld. I can't say I was weeping with sorrow when they disappeared.

At the beginning of two thousand and four I managed a trip back to Abu Dhabi to spend some time with my lovely friend, Helen. This was a positive time in my life. We drank and dined in the finest restaurants, worshipped the sun on beaches as white and unspoilt as pure silk, meandered around the lavish malls, with their extravagant displays of wealth and finesse and laughed until we cried with tears of unadulterated joy. I am certain the insane levels of sunlight in the Emirates had a positive effect on my mental health. I felt alive and joyous, fully of exceptional positivity and driven purpose.

On returning home, things gradually started to slip. The immense joy and positivity I'd felt on my recent holiday slowly corroded, my mask of normality metamorphosing into one of tearful neurosis. Little by little, my sanity began to drip away, precious drops of neurological normality, flowing away down the sewer of mental equilibrium. Psychosis and depression gradually seeped their way into my daily experience, sucking away at my sense of reality. In psychosis, what is not there is there, the unreal gains momentum until the real becomes polluted with a world of unreality and nonsense. The veil between reality and hallucination is very delicate, and to me, rapidly travelling at break neck speed to a date with psychiatric admission, disturbing and dark. The smell of gas would taunt and terrify me, and I would envision whole exaggerated scenarios of explosions and dramatic disasters. Electrical items terrified me and I became averse to touching anything of that nature. Obviously, these are utilities we cannot live without, so to have developed a total paranoid aversion to them was not only terrifying but distressing. I would shake with fear and trepidation, as my psychosis rendered me physically and mentally incapacitated.

I started having delusions about the leader of the occult group I had been a member of, in Manchester. She was using her powers to spy on me, to control my will, and she had the power to transform herself into different people. In my psychotic state, I firmly believed she had the power to 'shapeshift'. She was possessing the bodies of innocent people in order to make sure I was not betraying her group. My mental health rapidly deteriorated and I was admitted to hospital against my own will. I screamed and appealed and tried to leave the consulting room, but I found myself on a Section Three once again. I was exceptionally angry, in a desperate state of physical neglect and of wildly unsound mind as I was led to my physical prison ward yet again.

Weeks passed, my psychosis continued. I wandered around the ward like a lost soul, full of frustration and angst. Days seemed like eternal seas of nothingness and nights were prisoners of beseeching souls. I neglected my appearance, hair unwashed, unkempt and garments tainted rather beyond their grimy sell-by date. I sat comatose, a vacant and uncomprehending expression upon my flaccid face. Far too much flesh hung off my idle bones, my weight having ballooned beyond desirable proportions. My diet consisted mostly of tobacco, whilst I huddled in the corner, clutching the burning embers of my last smoke with yellowed, nicotine-stained fingers. I am not sure whether it was the drug itself or the ritualistic aspect that had got me hooked. Smoking on a psychiatric ward is one way to develop one's assertive skills. You have a precious commodity, your tobacco, which is highly sought after. Many patients have nothing to call their own, especially the luxury of cigarettes, so when you are sitting in the lounge with your packet of twenty, you become a beacon for beggars and scroungers, a shining light of addictive substance in an environment of deprivation. At first you are beset with kindness and generosity until you realise you have to be tough, and then you change. You get harder and more cynical, you learn to protect your assets and not let other patients take you for granted. We are taught in life to always be generous and kind, to be giving and sympathetic. It is not always as straight cut as that, sometimes you have to say enough is enough and not let anyone use you as a carpet.

I would wander the ward like a wailing banshee, swearing and cursing, screaming like a tortured prisoner, pleading for someone to help me. I went up to the nurses' station, adrenaline coursing through my veins, grabbed a chair and hurled it across the room with all my might. Everyone was stunned as I yanked up the table and turned it clean over, paperwork scattering around the station like wedding confetti. The nurses sprung to action and I was led to the seclusion room, a banal, beige, cushioned affair, devoid of any contents. It was a safe place, for both the patients and staff, a place where you could explode with the greatest shower of fury and rage, where you could flail and scream, yell obscenities to the furthest reaches of Hades, have a physical fight with your imaginary demons, yet still be contained safely. It was both a cool down room and a containment room, keeping nurses safe and patients protected from themselves and others. In the seclusion room I felt safe, not from other patients, but from myself. My mind had become my enemy, betraying me again and again with its diet of suicidal ideation and surreptitious self-destruction. Being in seclusion was a brief hiatus from the pressures of social acceptability, an oasis in the desert of psychological dis-function.

Sometimes the mental pressure was too much, and I desperately wanted to cause myself pain as a distraction process. Not too much pain and certainly not involving knives or blood! My modus operandi was to hold a lighter beneath my wrist, letting the heat accumulate and crescendo into a scorching, blistering climax. For a few blissful moments, the burning pain seared through my physical body, whilst my mind was free of its mental anguish.

I had previously been diagnosed as having bipolar disorder. This diagnosis was questioned during my stay on Ward Eighteen, where the psychiatrist was querying a diagnosis of schizophrenia. However, it was finally decided that I be given a diagnosis of schizoaffective disorder. Schizoaffective disorder has elements of both a mood disorder and schizophrenia. There may be episodes of severe depression or mania, along with psychotic symptoms such as hallucinations and delusions. Although I had experienced one major episode of mania, which lasted around eight or nine months, I had mostly experienced severe depression and psychosis, such as voices telling me to harm myself or others, delusions about strangers putting thoughts into my mind and other such things. I was not aware until many years later that I had been given this diagnosis in 2004. I had believed I had bipolar disorder. It wasn't until eight years later when I learnt the truth.

Eventually things started to improve, thanks to medication, the doctors' and nurses' patience and care and the support of my loving family. My late grandfather, then in his eighties was at my side throughout. Although he lived an hour's journey away, he would be beside me day in, day out, making me smile, infinitely patient and supportive. We would while away the hours in the patients' lounge, playing clumsily on the piano or potting a black on the pool table. He never judged my mental illness and was never ashamed of me. He was fiercely loyal and devoted to his family and for that I was grateful. My mother and sisters were always there for me. I am certain my mother is an Earth angel, for she is the kindest woman, with the greatest compassionate heart, that you could ever meet on our planet. I am blessed to know so much love for it has brought me through the darkest of times.

Finally, after periods of leave, whereby a patient gradually displays increasing levels of stability and trustworthiness, I was given discharge, the ultimate achievement as far as psychiatric hospitals go! I returned to my home and attempted to re-establish a modicum of normality in my then-crazy life.

'Domesticated? Me?'

Domesticated? Me?
Go ask the cupboard full of brushes,
Potions, gels, assorted
Evidence of good intentions.

Never was domestic goddess,
Flitzing, glitzing, blitzing,
Waving wand of pristine rightness,
No perfect make up glamour puss.

Pay homage to the women who
Established self-esteem upon
Crisp lines of pure white nappies,
Floating freshly on the gentle wind.

But they were bygone days of wifedom,
I, woman of now, no icon,
Sit, procrastinate a little,
Perhaps enjoy another coffee,
What's the rush, I sigh.

© *Sarah Drury*

TEN

Life had its challenges over the following year. I had spiraled into debt which was crippling me financially. Emotionally, I was exhausted with the worry of it all, hope cast aside as life's dramas deemed insurmountable. I was inundated with threatening mail from my creditors and rather than tackle things head on and rise to the challenge, I ran at lightning speed with my coward's tail between my knees. Madness slowly beckoned my presence, with its dark echoes of subtle unease seeping into my psyche.

My fascination with spiritual aspects of life took a fierce hold. I became fascinated by the occult and threw myself wholeheartedly into my spiritual pursuits. I became fascinated with crystals and signed myself up for a course in crystal healing. I became heavily involved with the group in Derbyshire, where we would immerse ourselves in meditation and metaphysical activity. We learned Reiki and would spend hours laying hands on each other in order to develop our skills. I really felt something special, really felt the energy pulsing through my hands. It was enlightening and liberating to feel part of something so alternative. We learned about reincarnation and the afterlife and I was totally convinced we were in touch with the dearly departed. I took a course in Reiki, passing my level I and took any opportunity to practice my skills on friends and family. I developed my tarot reading skills, although nowadays I have different beliefs. It was a gentle way of living, but my obsession became dark and all consuming. I started to have conversations with the dead and imagine their presence, hearing their voices and seeing visions of them. To this day I believe that we can contact our deceased relatives, and I also have great faith in the spiritual aspects of life. However, when it tips over the edge into dark obsession, it is not the best situation for somebody with a severe, psychotic mental illness. The boundaries between the physical world and the spiritual are very fine and sometimes indistinguishable. My mind embraced the surreal and I fell into a dark place.

I was admitted to the ward for another few months as I struggled to cope with reality. I suffered the same delusions, fought with the voices which tormented me and battled to drag myself, broken and wounded, gasping and heaving, from the depths of this ocean of unreality in which I had slowly drowned. Time is a great healer as they always say, and with time I slowly took little baby steps into a more sane, balanced landscape, with a mind working on a more rational level.

I was not aware at the time, but my whole world was about to explode in a kaleidoscope of passion and excitement and my life would never be the same again. My computer was a blessed friend, the holy grail of online romance as I accidently met my knight in shining armour on social media, and instantly fell head over heels in love. Soon we were emailing with a heady passion and the magic was undeniable, a chemistry so powerful we had to meet.

The morning of our first meeting, the air was alive with unspoken possibility. I flitted around like a demented butterfly, unable to settle my heart or my mind. I had on my finest attire, and my immaculately made up face beamed with a happiness that matched the passion of my crimson-lipped smile. Every car which approached caused the net curtains to twitch a little, as my eager eyes surveyed the street for signs of the golden chariot that would carry my beloved to his destination. Finally, his little blue Vauxhall pulled outside the house and the air around me swelled with expectation. I didn't wait for the knock, I just flung the door open and threw my arms around this wonderful human standing before me, this gentle, kind, romantic prince of my heart. It was love in an instant. We immediately connected, and we spoke the same, silent, timeless language of deep soul connection.

Meeting John changed my life in so many ways. It put me on a new, more positive pathway and as I slowly learned the meaning of true love, my soul was gradually healing. The depression eased, and my life became balanced and joyful. The love of another human being is the most powerful potion that exists and to be enwrapped in its tender wings is so beautiful and special. I learned to live life with meaning again, to take pleasure in being in a warm, supportive partnership, healing each other, taking each precious moment and making the best of it. We enjoyed our happy days, two people in love, soothing each other's troubles. We had a rich social life, made many new friends. We would spend happy times in the local club, John playing darts and I singing. We lived for today, happily and with contentment.

There was a dark shadow looming and it was John's deteriorating health. He had a serious heart condition and had been given early retirement from his job as a tree surgeon, which broke his heart. I was optimistic in the beginning and didn't predict the tremendous impact it would have on our lives. I was naïve, but I loved this man with the core of my being, so would stand by him through thick or thin. One morning, I went into the bedroom to find John breathless and in terrible pain. He could not speak nor express himself. The ambulance came quickly and rushed him to the emergency department. I could hear his desperation from the little relatives' room, a room I now dread. His heart was failing and the doctors were battling desperately. I waited, stunned and silent, not realising this was a blip compared to what lay ahead. Time stood still as he clung onto life with all of his soul. It was not his time to leave us, and after a few days in the medical assessment unit he was able to return to me.

We lived life to the fullest, fully aware of the limitations of my beloved's heart. We walked hand-in-hand along the promenade at Cleethorpes, gazing into each other's eyes like the love birds that we were, two souls connecting through loving hearts. This man was therapy, he took my fragmented mind and tenderly nurtured it into a state of mindful wholeness. He banished the demons from my tortured psyche, not through violence but through unconditional love.

Life was sweet and simple for a while, but there was news coming which would turn our blissful, leisurely world upside down! I stood in the bathroom gazing at the shocking truth held in my hand, a mixture of electricity and sheer dread. This couldn't be true. Not now. I was going to be a mother, at the age of 38 years. I, mentally unstable since the age of 30, was going to bring forth a precious soul, the most sacred gift in the universe. I was fearful and exhilarated.

I stood in front of my beloved, holding the test stick in my shaky fingers. At first, John thought it was some kind of prank. He was incredulous and at first felt negative about the whole situation. As he saw it, he had a life limiting heart condition and I had a serious mental illness. How on earth could it possibly work. There was a lot of heart searching that week and I decided to have an early pregnancy scan. It was the most uplifting thing that had ever happened to me, the moment I saw my baby, a tiny little foetus, on the screen. His little fluttering butterfly heart determined this tiny little soul's survival and touched both of our lives for eternity.

Pregnancy was a treacherous ordeal physically. My psychiatrist insisted I stay on my mood stabilisers, as the risk of deterioration was great, and I needed to be sane right now. I had a commitment to my precious unborn child, to be the best mother I could possibly be. There were people who seriously questioned my ability to be a successful parent and I couldn't blame them. I had hardly proved responsible and balanced over the last 10 years. I had my teaching experience behind me, which proved I could be motherly, but could I defy my genetics and stay in control of my mind and sanity.

I suffered from gestational diabetes and intense morning sickness but thankfully, my mental health remained stable. I had never been happier, nurturing a precious new life within and loved unconditionally by the most gentle, kind and generous man I'd ever known. Gentle, yes, but dependable and unbreakable. Pregnancy was an uneventful period of my life, with many fond memories of blissful times. I was floating in a bubble of euphoria and it was heavenly.

A Mother's Love

My sweet most precious treasure
Purest heart of innocence,
A million dragons, jaws of fiery rage
All cowered rapt in mercy
Scorched and charred, no match
So powerful is the love I hold
For you, My son.

My pure, dear, tender man child,
Sweetest lips of sugared gossamer,
A thousand witches, ranting wildly, wicked,
Hellfire burning, chants a screeching,
Shriveled, spellbound, cast beyond,
No match for full heart
Of a mother's love, my child.

My darling, dear heart youth,
Precious eyes of tourmaline,
A hundred monsters, ravenous and jawing
Clawing, flesh-hunt crawling,
Banished into kingdom come
By the fearsome hunger of
A mother's love, my son.

My cherished, loving one,
Shimmering halo of iridescence,
A trillion kisses, a billion wishes
Of sweetness and sugar and candy floss fluffiness,
Angels on cupcakes in clouds of marshmallow,
Here lies the story, the kingdom, the power,
A mother's love, my son.
© *Sarah Drury*

ELEVEN

I lay on the bed, a sheet veiling the nether regions of my bloated physique. I was shaking with anticipation. The atmosphere was intense. A plethora of green-clad medics surrounded me as I called out for my husband, who was desperately throwing on his green scrubs. He burst into the operating theatre just as the surgeon raised the glinting scalpel, slicing through my abdomen with skill and precision. I longed to hear the cry of my son, as he gasped his first breath, fresh out of the security and comfort of his watery dwelling. I had longed for this day, had envisioned the beauty and emotion as my child was placed in my arms and we gazed contentedly into each-other's dewy eyes.

The minutes ticked by and the mood darkened and became sombre. I began to fear the worst as my son was quietly taken to a corner of the room for resuscitation. I was desperate to know what was happening. Why had no-one uttered a word to me, comforted me, reassured me? Was my child alive? Was he breathing?

After a lengthy ordeal, my son, completely wrapped in blankets, apart from his little face, was presented to me for a precious fleeting moment, before he was whisked away into the NICU, or Neonatal Intensive Care Unit. I had one precious keepsake to keep me close to my beautiful, newborn son. A single photograph of him basking contentedly in the warmth of his incubator in the NICU. I kept that photo close to my heart as I was confined to the prison of my hospital bed. It was twenty-four hours before I finally cradled my precious new bundle in my delighted arms. I vowed in my heart to protect this miracle and to dedicate my life to nurturing him with every ounce of stability and unconditional love I had within my soul.

It was a week before we were allowed home, and Milo, my son, had made a full recovery. He was a robust, sturdy child who was very vocal. He made our world complete and we doted on this cherished little human as though he was a tiny prince. As he grew we started to notice that his development was slightly delayed. At this point it was not a great concern, though as he grew older it had implications for his psychological and emotional development.

Throughout the whole time, I had maintained a positive and stable mentality. It was as though my illness was miraculously cured, by sheer love and contentment. My beloved partner was an antidote to madness, and my son was a powerful antidepressant. There were some slight dark clouds on the horizon, mainly the troubling debts and financial instabilities which I had accumulated through my mania and lack of insight. I made a life changing decision to sell my house and relocate to the city of Hull, across the River Humber.

The move went smoothly and although we had less space, there were many positives about our new location. My husband had access to excellent medical resources, which would prove vital over the coming years, as my husband battled desperately with his severe heart condition.

We were close to my husband's family, which was comforting for my husband and of great support during difficult times.

Life continued on a positive path, and Milo stayed relatively strong and healthy. However, his developmental delay became extremely apparent by the age of two, and he was referred to the psychologist for assessment. By the age of two and a half, he began attending a special school in the nearby village of Welton. He had no speech, would barely eat, and had no interest in playing with toys. My husband and I loved him wholeheartedly and accepted his differences with love and determination to get him the help and support he needed.

In the meantime, my husband's health deteriorated drastically. He was spending periods of time in the heart unit at Castle Hill Hospital, where he had several close calls with death. I do not know where we both found the strength to endure the hardship of the unpredictability and severity of his condition. We made a decision to marry in April 2010. It was the happiest day of our lives as we gazed into each other's eyes, and recited words of commitment to one another surrounded by our loved ones. Little did we know our time was tragically limited, and we are not always winners in the lottery that is life.

The year following our wedding was tumultuous. My husband became desperately ill and truly fought for his precious life. The doctors diagnosed that they could do nothing more, and wanted to withdraw treatment, to my great distress. One very determined ward sister managed to overturn this decision and my husband was placed on life support, where he remained for many weeks. When he recovered, whilst on the ward, he had a stroke. This left him severely incapacitated and needing rehabilitation for many more weeks. When he finally came home he had a brain haemorrhage resulting in more treatment. After spending a few months at home, he became desperately ill again and was transferred to the Freeman Hospital in Newcastle. They did everything they could to save my husband. He was encapsulated within a small room full of incredible technology, and machines which bleeped and flashed and performed miraculous feats. They were keeping my husband alive, and for that I was grateful. My husband was fitted with a mechanical heart to take the pressure off his own failing organ. I would sit dutifully by his side, my own heart breaking at the sight of this beautiful and strong man, fighting for survival. He appeared to make progress, although was not lucid during the last week of his life.

In the meantime, my grandfather passed away, sadly, and I came back to attend his funeral. Little did I know the events that were going to unfold. After the ceremony, I received a phone call from the hospital informing me that my husband had taken a turn for the worse and was on life support. I frantically made the four-hour journey, by train, to Newcastle, my heart pounding and my mind a quagmire of terror and desperation. On arriving at the hospital, I was able to sit with my husband, but the news wasn't what I'd been wanting to hear. My husband had haemorrhaged severely. They had operated to drain the blood, but he had haemorrhaged once again and there was nothing more they could do to save him. My heart and spirit broke, as the nurse in charge of his care asked for permission to turn off his life-support.

I sat beside my darling husband, poised and composed, preparing for his last moments. It was the most surreal experience, like being in a heart-wrenching true movie. The nurse asked me, quietly, was I ready and I nodded gently, poised and composed, whilst inside I was broken and devastated. The artificial heart ticked loudly, flooding the room with its forlorn echo, then abruptly it halted and there was just a deafening silence. Time came to a standstill, as my beautiful husband was at last at peace.

I, and both of our families, were completely devastated by the loss of this incredibly strong, gentle, kind and devoted man we had had the fortune to have shared our lives with. My son was just three and a half years old. Our lives had changed in the blink of an eye, and a new chapter had been written.

'The Veil'

I gaze beseechingly upon you, my love,
With no mere mortal gaze, nor eyes no longer sapphire blue,
I see your tears cascade,
Deep oceans ebb in rhythm with
Your yearning heart so pure, so true.
I touch, so gently, reaching for that face forlorn,
With no mere mortal hand, nor fingers earthly tangible.
I feel your heart awash with grief,
The wind is wildly howling, singing of your heart so full.
I hear, so clearly, whispering back in gossamer tones,
With no mere mortal ears, nor strident voice of earthly throes.
I sing your sounds, I hear your pain,
My every word a delicate flower, a pure white rose.
I wait, tenderly, just beyond the veil, my dear,
With no mere mortal heart, only devoted soul,
My love, the heart-told language in this other realm,
Communion, reunion,
two eager hearts at last made whole.

© *Sarah Drury*

TWELVE

After three years of relative equilibrium, my mind balanced and focused on the love and contentment I had known, the shadows amassed in the deep, dark, recesses of my troubled mind. My coping mechanisms had crumbled into dust. I battled through each day, the bereaved widow that I now was, as though my life was a barren, war-stricken landscape, perpetually dark and desecrated. My mind began to disintegrate, as my untarnished life slowly unraveled.

I missed my husband so desperately, I could not imagine life without him by my dutiful side. I longed to hear his dulcet voice, the heartfelt laughter, the light-hearted banter and the words of comfort and support that this loving man would always share. He was my sanctuary and kept me sane. His love was more powerful than any medication the psychiatrist could have prescribed. I had felt truly valued and my sense of worth made me see that I was more than a diagnosis, more than a chapter in a psychiatric journal. But this was slowly slipping, ebbing away into a pool of disenchantment and self-disrespect.

Milo had been diagnosed with autism and his behaviour could be quite challenging. He was barely able to walk or talk and had many sensory issues. I was finding it increasingly difficult to exist, day-to-day, in any normal capacity. I was under the care of the mental health team in Hull and had a CPN (community psychiatric nurse), who oversaw my well-being and monitored my mental state. I was at crisis point as I sat face-to-face with this gentle, kind hearted lady, and shattered into a million fragments of sadness and dysfunction. It was time for me to seek respite in hospital once again. I was beside myself with self-loathing and repugnance, but could no longer hold myself above the turbulent waters of my psyche.

With a heavy heart I carried my small bundle of meagre belongings to my sparse, characterless room in the mental health unit. It had been a few years now since I saw the four walls of such a place, and the self-hate I felt was unprecedented. Processing my new environment was distressing and tormenting. I wanted to hide away from society, and myself. I was angst ridden and ready to implode. I desensitised myself from my surroundings and for a couple of days shut myself away like a recluse. I then peered through the curtains of civilisation and ventured into my disturbing reality.

There were some characters in the unit. My memory is very limited as I was extremely distressed, but I met a girl of African descent who also had bipolar disorder. She was a boisterous extrovert with many psychological issues. She was an avid self-harmer and deeply insecure. We became friends, although friendship in the psychiatric unit is most always tainted by underlying tragedy and mutual suffering. She had a passion for music, most notably Nicki Minaj, and would blare out music at a magnified rate of decibels, whilst we both gyrated to the beat. One night, we were sitting in her room when out of nowhere she brandished a razor blade and started slicing deeply into her calves! The crimson blood oozed out onto the floor and all over her legs and feet. The nurses came tearing into the room and ushered me out of that dark situation. I was repulsed by what I had seen and especially by the light-hearted, frivolous manner in which she had disfigured herself. I had always imagined that to self-harm, one must come from a place deeply dark and tormented. But psychiatric illness has many faces and many motivations.

I was transferred to the long stay unit where I had a more private room. Although I was depressed, I was bored, tormented and disturbed, with no real outlet for my frustration. My mood was fluctuating between desperately hopeless and hypomanic. I would punish myself by inflicting minor pain and discomfort, such as burning myself with a lighter, but this was more as a distraction from my psychological disturbance than a real desire to self-mutilate.

I met some interesting people in that unit. Janice, a slight, manic, black woman was a real character. She spoke and moved at breakneck speed, twitching and gesticulating wildly the whole time. She fluctuated between aggression and extreme hospitality, depending on her rapidly changing mood. She would inspect the floors with a hawk's eye, searching for 'tab ends', the discarded cigarettes that littered the floor of the smoking area. She would disappear into the city and return with bags upon bags of new clothes, another symptom of the excesses of mania.

Stacey, a short, stout lady, who seemed very level headed and sensible, was chronically depressed and had attempted suicide multiple times, but had so far been unsuccessful. She was desperately disillusioned with life and existence and was ready to leave the world behind. She was deeply unhappy, but her outward appearance betrayed her fragile and dark mental state. She was a good friend to me whilst I was in that unit and always seem so stable.

Another lady who touched my heart was Eileen. Once an attractive and successful wife and mother, her life had plunged into one of extreme anxiety and disassociation. No longer understanding who she was, and crippled with fear and insecurity, this lady would wander round the garden, muttering inaudibly in the language that was impossible to comprehend. She would plead for cigarettes from the other patients and would have smoked herself into an early grave if the nurses hadn't curtailed her requests. It was heart-breaking to see how shattered and disassociated she was, a mere shadow of her former, fully functioning self. I often wonder what became of the people who touched my life for these brief moments of time. Did they continue to suffer the rest of their lives? Did they even continue to live? Did they succumb to the darkness in their souls? Or did they soar above and beyond their crippling mental condition towards a positive and therapeutic happy ending.

I was blessed to be surrounded by loving family members who would visit and lift my sorry spirit. My husband's sisters, who had always accepted and supported my husband and I through the darkest of hours, and my immediate family, my beautiful mother, selfless with a heart as big as the universe, and my two wonderful sisters, with whom I have laughed in the face of enormous adversity. I was ashamed to allow them to see me in my distressed, disheveled and unbalanced state of weakness. I had become an unkempt shadow of my previous, serene self, loitering about like a creature of the night, lurking amidst the black crevices of my shattered psyche. I felt like the most terrible, neglectful, insane mother to a child who himself had additional needs due to his autism. My son was staying with my mother whilst I was suffering, and there he had a happy, calm and nurturing environment, which I was unable to give him at that harrowing time.

My mother has been a beautiful angel throughout my whole illness, and always been there to support me, loving me no matter how bizarre and extreme my behaviour was. I missed my son terribly and was determined to grasp life with every ounce of strength I could muster. I could not fail my husband, my son needed me, and I needed my sanity to return.

Eventually I was granted discharge and decided to return to the home of my parents, where I could be with my son and regain my shattered confidence and dissipated sense of self. I slept on the sofa and concentrated on building the delicate relationship with my beautiful son. Time passed, and my strength gradually increased to the point where I was able to rent a little house in the same village as my mother.

The house met our needs very well and was a stable home for my son and I for a year or two. Life was not without its problems. Milo's autism exhibited itself in many ways, but the most difficult was definitely his meltdowns. A meltdown is a situation where an autistic child becomes extremely agitated and upset to the point of screaming and crying. The child loses control and can lash out and become violent. These were a frequent occurrence in our lives and it has taken me many years to become calm and patient when in such a situation. Milo had started a new specialist school in Scunthorpe and was making great progress there. For a child who had had such a traumatic start in life, he was remarkably content and seemingly well-balanced. He didn't understand about his father and had little memory of him. I always tried to keep his memory alive through browsing family photographs and encouraging Milo to talk to his daddy in heaven. We were happy in the house for a year, but things were soon to change.

THIRTEEN

The first sign of euphoria seeped into my consciousness around the early summer of 2012. I had begun to feel exceptionally positive and highly stimulated, in denial of my previous anxiety and depression. Life had become a colossal adventure, not a second to be wasted on the trivial or mundane. I was barely sleeping nor eating, and would spend every evening browsing the Internet, whilst Milo slept soundly. It was there that I discovered new age spirituality. I was immediately hooked, and it became entrenched in every breath I took and every thought that burst through my mind. I became obsessed with its ideas and teachings and these were soon to take over my whole being. I began to meditate twice a day, and was desperate to experience a spiritual awakening. I truly thought that I would suddenly transform into a perfect and unworldly being with immense psychic powers!

I happened upon a guy who was spiritual teacher, and frequented his website and forum for discussion. It became my second virtual home, and I would relish every word that was posted and every concept that was introduced. I became completely obsessed with the man himself and was convinced that this was a meeting of heavenly souls which was written in the annals of time. I truly believed that we were meant to be together as 'Twin Souls'. (A Twin Soul is two people who are half of a single unit, two souls who belong together). I started to believe that this fine gentleman, who happens to be a very trustworthy and genuine person, was visiting me in spirit. I believed our souls were forever entwined. I lived on the forums, truly believing the jumbled words which were spewing forth from my fingers, in response to the deluded and psychotic processes in my mind.

The psychosis took a hold and the spiritual world became very real. I would feel the undeniably sexual touch of an invisible hand and hear the voice of a man who had no physical presence, caressing me with his dulcet, rich tones. Huge currents of electricity would flood my body, leaving me tingling and ecstatic. I would see dark shadows lurking in corners, though my psychosis had led me to believe that I was fully in touch with the spirit world and had nothing to fear. One night I was in my bedroom, meditating, when a male voice ordered me to look in the mirror and I would see the ladies in the moon Temple of Atlantis where I was once a servant. I got down on my knees as I listened to the commanding voice. When looking in the mirror I was faced with a beautiful vision of an incredible marble temple full of nubile young women, the moon above shining resplendently as it was dutifully worshipped. To me these phenomena seemed as tangible as the physical world, and as I gradually lost touch with reality, the veil between the seen and the unseen eventually dissipated.

Our house inexplicably became invaded with house flies. Well, there were several anyway. My sister wanted to kill them with spray, but I believed with all my heart that they were incarnations of spirits who had passed, and were my friends. I would merrily talk to them, and they became my guests.

Music became a huge feature of my life at that chaotic time. The music channels were on tv constantly, as the current hits blared out repeatedly. Each song had a special meaning in my life, being a significant and particular part of my life events. I believed that the lyrics were specifically about me, a narcissistic trait that can be common during mania or psychosis. Was my life dictating the music, or was the music dictating my life? I became completely immersed, and would spend hours submerged in the melodies and lyrics. There was one particular song, 'Spectrum', by Florence and the Machine, that took on a particular significance. I believed it was about reincarnation, specifically my past life as the goddess Isis. By the end of this period, I truly believed that there was a conglomerate of female artists, singing and creating music all about my life!

The psychosis was not in the slightest traumatic, and had no negativity about it, not until the end, when the darkness descended, and my illness took a tragic turn. My life for a while was cloaked in a beautiful radiance of fantasy, where the impossible became my reality. It was a fantastical time, and although my sanity is my most precious commodity, I am grateful that, for a brief moment in time, I was able to live in a land where anything was possible.

Throughout this crazy time, I was fully able to care for my son and meet all of his needs. Living in such a fantastical state of mind, I was able to channel this into my parenting and create a little make-believe with my child. On one occasion we had a trip to Cleethorpes, the seaside resort not far from my home. It was an exciting day and a magical experience. We went on the beach, had tasty fish and chips, Milo rode the rides, but the magical part was a walk along the promenade. My psychosis had taken a religious bent. I had begun to believe that I was the incarnation of the Virgin Mary. I believed this with every ounce of my being. I believed I was special and that Milo, my son, was an incarnation of Jesus Christ. He was special, and his magnificence radiated from the centre of his soul into the world beyond. As we walked along the promenade, Milo shone, and I sensed that people could feel his specialness and godliness. He was, after all, religious royalty. The walk was grandiose, and one lady even stopped to look at us and say how special Milo was, which nourished my delusions of grandeur. In the gift shop, Milo chose a great sword, which led to me to believe that he was Archangel Michael. How he could change so quickly from one incarnation to another would prove confusing for most normal individuals, but to my psychotic mind, anything was conceivable.

Part of the teachings of the New Age movements are that we create our reality through our thoughts. Positive thoughts will create positive situations. Likewise, negative thoughts will create negative situations. We are all innate creators, all miniature gods and goddesses in our own right. Although this is still my belief, at that time my mind was fragmenting, and my thoughts were becoming more extreme and bizarre. I started to fear every thought that I had, believing that it was going to bring forth doom and catastrophe. I believed I was in control of the weather, that I had influence on world events and tragedies. This was a very heavy burden for a sensitive lady like myself. I began to live a life of unease and trepidation. Anxiety sneaked in between the delusions of grandeur and the increasingly dark thought processes. I was starting to unravel, to slip beneath the radar of my previous positive attitude. I sat, one day, in meditation, when a sudden darkness froze my soul and threw me into a frightening state of agitation and abject terror. I became completely distressed and sat screaming and crying, repenting my sins. I then stripped naked and believed I was a moon goddess. The moon was gleaming through the curtainless window, as I stood basking in its splendour, tears of desperation trickling down my dewy cheek, like the caress of a fallen angel.

It was inevitable that, at this low ebb, I would be taking a much-abhorred trip to the psych ward once again. I had lost all touch with reality by the time I arrived at the hospital. I was inhabiting my own fantasy realm, unfettered by the restraints of physical existence. I sat, unresponsive and unintelligible, on the seats near the nurses' station, gazing into nothingness and laughing hysterically with no stimulus for my apparent hilarity. Beside me sat my patient and humble CPN, Sara, forever calm and understanding, whatever my state of being. We sat a while, me unresponsive and trapped somewhere in my psychosis, Sara just comforting me, a voice of reason. I was gently led to my own private room, a smart if rather barren environment, which afforded me some much-needed privacy. For several days I sought sanctity in my aloneness, refusing to interact with the reality which threatened my sense of security. Reality was my detested enemy yet also the ultimate destination of my recovery; redemption through submitting to treatment and medication, two things which seemed, at the time, immense threats.

I became increasingly anxious as the days moved on, and would either ensconce myself in my little room, away from the confusion and pandemonium of the bustling ward, or would pace the corridors, pleading for an end to the mental confusion and torment which predominated my conscious mind, making every moment a humongous hurdle to negotiate. I was extremely wary of the other patients, terrified of the unpredictability and eccentricity of their behaviour. It is very difficult, when an inpatient of a psychiatric ward, to cope with the illness of another when you are, yourself, so fragile and vulnerable. For me, it initially created a chasm which repelled me from interacting with other patients through fear and distrust. I find that this barrier eventually breaks down, the stronger you feel. Slowly, you take baby steps to overcome your fears and begin to integrate into the routine of the ward. The routine becomes your comfort blanket and you take solace in its regularity and structure. It doesn't change and is constant. You become familiar with the patients faces, gradually, perhaps even interacting a little; a quick hello, maybe even sharing a smoke. You learn to navigate the various nuances of the other patients' behaviour, to anticipate their quirks and responses so as not to provoke a negative response. I remember there was an elderly lady who was having a psychosis and did not respond to efforts to converse. I took pity on her and made her a cup of tea. She uttered three little words: "Thank you queen". I was still in partial psychosis and this heightened my delusion of grandeur. I already believed I was the virgin Mary and now I was also a queen! Part of my psychosis led me to believe that I was expecting a holy child through way of immaculate conception. I had not had a sexual relationship since my husband had died the year before, so it was inconceivable that I could possibly be pregnant. But to my confused mind, I bore the child who would be the second coming of Jesus Christ! I was exceptionally disappointed when the pregnancy test was negative, and my delusion was shattered.

Eventually, my delusions receded, and my tired mind established itself in the phenomenon that is the real, physical existence. I returned home to my empty little house, whilst my son stayed with my dear mother. I spent most of my time at my mother's, with my beautiful son, as my own home felt devoid of love and comfort. He had settled well. In the meantime, social services had become involved and were doubtful for my son's wellbeing under my care. I can understand the reasons why, as I had a severe mental illness, but I was a very proud lady who had a very strong bond with her only child. There were many visits from the social worker, and much consternation when I announced that I was going to take my son back home for weekends. Permission was granted, but I was heavily monitored. In the meantime, my mother was given parental responsibility, in the event that I was unable to care for my son, permanently or temporarily. I was very grateful for the love and support my mother had shown us both. She is the most generous, loving and non-judgemental person I have ever know, and I am truly blessed to be her daughter.

Time passed, and my son came home permanently. I was the best mother I could ever be. Never again would I allow myself to sink beyond the veil and threaten everything I loved and cared for, passionately. I had come so close to losing everything, including my own sanity. My son was my world, the most precious gift I had ever been blessed with. I owed it to my husband to give my child and I a bright future, the happiness and security we both deserved.

Aged only 5

My darling child, my heart and soul,
You dream oh so sweetly,
Your breath soft and gentle,
Swaddled in soft duvets,
And blessed with unconditional love.
You light up my world
Like the brightest of fires,
You are that twinkling star,
The world's brightest diamond.
Sleep hushly, little one,
Treasure your days of innocence.
Enjoy the adoration of your love-smitten mother,
Of days of laughter and frolicsome joy,
Of lollipops and chocolate mice
And teddy bears picnics.
Dance in the light of your highest dreams
Because you are so loved, little one,
So very treasured my beautiful son.
I – love – you.

© *Sarah Drury*

FOURTEEN

After a short while, we moved in with my mother due to problems with the heating at our then current home. It was overcrowded, but we were warm and fed and happy. A house came up for rent across from my mother, so we took the lease and moved in shortly after. It was rather a ramshackle house, decrepit and unsightly. It was also cold and draughty due to poor insulation and badly fitting doors and windows. The décor was shabby and displeasing to the eye. My mother tried her hardest to add some colour and comfort, but I never had the motivation to tackle the larger jobs. We made it our home for a while, and during the warm, pleasant summer months, it was tolerable.

My mood stayed fairly stable during the time that we lived there, but there was another dark cloud rapidly gaining presence at an alarming rate. I had become anxious over the slightest hiccups which was tolerable at first, as I was able to rationalise my fears. I had been under an enormous amount of stress over the previous couple of years and this was bound to take its toll. I became fixated on household utilities, particularly the electricity and oil. I became obsessed that there was going to be an electrical fire of some sort. I would forever be desperately checking the plug sockets to ensure they were switched off whenever it was bedtime or if I had to leave the house. If I left the house, I would have to go back several times to ensure they were actually turned off. This was interfering with my daily routine enormously and also causing distress to the point that I was afraid to leave the house or go to sleep.

Perpetuating these bothersome fears were the left-over delusions of my previous psychosis. I believed that my thoughts created my reality, and to have such negative beliefs and then to constantly assume that these negative contemplations would manifest in reality, was crippling and alarming. The tiniest, negative thought would trigger a cycle of fear and apprehension, which eventually became unbearable.

I opened up to Sara, my psychiatric nurse, and was referred to the psychologist for counselling and a course of treatment. It was felt that I would benefit from some grief counselling. The therapist was a lovely young woman, and immediately put me at ease. We discussed my husband's tragic and untimely death and explored how I genuinely felt, beneath the heroic façade. We worked though my phobias, using a mixture of mindfulness and probability diagrams and concepts. I learnt how to put my fears into context and see the wider viewpoint. After many weeks of therapy, I was able to cope a little better with those nasty, intrusive patterns within my unsettled mind, and move onto more settled shores.

By July of 2014, we moved into a lovely little home in a quiet cul-de-sac. We were surrounded by fields and countryside, and had great neighbours who were extremely supportive and understanding of Milo's condition. Life became more settled than it had ever been during the last four years, and we fell into a solid routine. My mental health stayed surprisingly stable for a couple of years. Life buzzed along merrily. My mood stayed level and life was as calm as a light summer's breeze, floating across a paradise island, in the warmth of the blazing sun. Milo was growing into an intelligent, fun-loving young fellow, and the meltdowns were happening less and less. We were really settled in our home, just the two of us.

In October of 2016, I felt the familiar buzz return, as life took on an exaggerated vibrancy, and my energy levels soared to excessive proportions. I became eternally optimistic, and my personality expansive. My enthusiasm for social activity soared, and my Facebook presence tripled. I began to spend excessively, splashing out thousands on new clothes and beauty products, all from the catalogue. I would model my new outfits on Facebook and Instagram, and became completely self-obsessed. I felt so good, riding high on a wave of pure narcissism, with a sprinkle of mania to make the recipe particularly potent. I ordered thousands of pounds worth of goods on credit – a new, expensive camera, a huge smart TV, a laptop, expensive camera lenses. I could not stop myself, I was caught in a loop of manic consumerism and it was dragging me at warp speed into a desperate place of debt and poverty.

After four months, the exuberant mood diminished, and I was extremely fortunate that I wasn't swallowed by a pit of darkest despair, as can happen after a prolonged episode of mania. I had amassed a huge amount of debt (about fifteen thousand pounds' worth) and was struggling to keep up with repayments to my creditors. I paid my debts with little left over for frivolities. By the time May came around, I decided to take steps to handle my finances more positively, and I signed up for a debt management plan.

FIFTEEN

It is the day of my forty-eighth birthday as I write this concluding chapter. I sit here, in a warm house, with food in the fridge and my beautiful son by my side, and feel thankful that I have my life, my home, my friends and my family. I have been free from psychosis for five years, and have managed to stay out of the dreaded psychiatric ward for just as long.

I owe my sanity to the wonder drug that has kept the disturbing darkness, and soaring manias, from my door. That drug is lithium. It has given me back my life, and I am forever grateful. Earlier in my illness, I was reluctant to take medication. I felt it destroyed the positive feelings and emotions, leaving me moronic and empty, like a lifeless victim of Dracula. I didn't realise that to have perpetual feelings of euphoria was not a natural state to be in, and that the medication merely normalised my moods. To feel 'normal' is something that takes a while to become accustomed to, as for someone with a mood disorder, it is difficult to comprehend what that exactly is. I know that different medications suit different people, and that no two people are alike. I also understand that when you are feeling poorly, and not in control of your moods or mental processes, then taking medication may be a huge problem. But from the bottom of my heart, I can say that if it wasn't for the lithium I take daily, I probably would no longer be here.

Mental illness can have enormous negative effects on a person's family or social situation. It is not easy to cope with a person with a severe psychiatric illness, and to become estranged must be a common situation. I am very fortunate that my family have always been there for me, supporting and caring for me in my darkest hours. My mother making the trip to Manchester every week just for a few hours visit with her exhausting, manic daughter, and my late grandfather making a four-hour round trip to visit me every evening, even in his mid-eighties! Friends may go by the wayside, but the people who truly love and care for you are the ones to cherish.

If there is one thing that suffering from a psychiatric illness teaches you, it's how to be humble. Society looks down on the mentally ill, in general. If you have a mental illness, not a lot is expected of you, really. People are very judgmental and disapproving. I learned that the day the ward sister turned to me, during an episode of mania, and said "People like you should never have children,". I hate, to this day, people labelling me as 'disabled' as I feel I am incredibly able, I just have an illness. But you do not have to live up to their lack of expectations for your future. Having a mental illness is not a death sentence. With the correct treatment, it can hopefully be managed. My illness certainly has positives, like the hypomanic phases where I can be super productive, and the creative forces I feel when my mood is soaring. I also know what it feels like to be down on my knees begging for life to be kind to me, and would never look down upon anyone at all.

If you asked me, "If you had the choice to take away your illness, would you?", I would say yes and no. Yes, because it tore my life apart at an early age and all my aspirations were shattered. No, because it has given me great compassion, patience and insight, and made me value the precious, simple things in life. Its fire burns within me, driving forth my creativity and passion to survive. I will continue to survive and beat this illness, day by day, as I choose life! And life is beautiful!

Visit from an Angel

An angel came to me last night,
Crept silently
Through skies so black
The moon and stars were lost
Amidst a sea of darkest ebony.
A touch upon my cheek,
A gentle warm caress,
So soft, a million feathers
Brushing, sweeping, floating,
Sweetest wings of gentleness.
My heart, a joyful vessel,
Touched, such tender passion,
Thousand glorious sunbeams
Radiant, jubilant heart,
Such sweetness,
Breathes the love of heaven.

© Sarah Drury

Printed in Great Britain
by Amazon